STILL SPEAKING ILL *of the* DEAD

More Jerks in Montana History

D1016843

STILL SPEAKING ILL *of the* DEAD

More Jerks in Montana History

Edited by Jon Axline and Jodie Foley

Contributing Authors
Jon Axline • Ellen Baumler • Jodie Foley
Kristin L. Gallas • Angie Gifford
Lyndel Meikle • Dave Walter

TWODOT®

GUILFORD, CONNECTICUT
HELENA, MONTANA

AN IMPRINT OF THE GLOBE PEQUOT PRESS

A · T W O D O T® · B O O K

Library of Congress Cataloging-in-Publication Data
Still speaking ill of the dead : more jerks in Montana history / edited
  by Jon Axline and Jodie Foley ; contributing authors, Jon Axline ...
  [et al.].— 1st ed.
    p. cm.
  Includes index.
  ISBN 0-7627-3624-0
  1. Montana—History—Anecdotes. 2. Montana—Biography—
Anecdotes. 3. Rogues and vagabonds—Montana—Biography—
Anecdotes. 4. Criminals—Montana—Biography—Anecdotes.
I. Axline, Jon. II. Foley, Jodie, 1964-

F731.6.S75 2005
978.6—dc22   2004060577

Manufactured in the United States of America
First Edition/First Printing

Contents

Acknowledgments

The authors and editors of this volume have many to thank—archivists, librarians, county clerks, clerks of court, and forbearing loved ones. However the very idea of "Jerks in Montana History" must be given our highest gratitude. For more than twenty-five years Dave Walter has presided over the "Jerks in Montana History" sessions of the annual Montana History Conference. With puns and humor at the ready, he has introduced modern-day Montanans to a host of crooks, misfits, and ne'er-do-wells—reminding us at each stage that history is not hero worship. As the creator and nurturer of these popular conference sessions, Dave provides an example of how historians should comport themselves . . . acknowledging biases and shortcomings, meticulously researching all possible resources, and never taking himself too seriously. In addition to all this, Dave generously offered his time and expertise to the authors during the research and writing of these essays. For all he has done to make this book possible, the authors humbly thank Dave—and we vow never to nominate him as an entry in any future volumes in this series.

The authors also wish to thank the Montana Historical Society and its peerless staff for providing extensive research assistance to each author and a venue for presenting their work. The research center and photograph archives provide a world of resources relating to jerks. Montana doesn't seem at a loss for candidates, but they are not always easy to find. The staff provides great access and assistance and often suggests nominees. We are grateful for their expertise and good humor.

Finally, a thank-you must be extended to each of the jerks in this volume. Their lives provide the backdrop for the larger story of Montana—a story that like them is complex, messy, and just plain interesting.

Introduction

Welcome to the second volume of *Speaking Ill of the Dead: Jerks in Montana History*. If history is any indicator, being bad is much more desirable than being good . . . at least for the people highlighted in this book. History is full of role models, some of good behavior and others of bad behavior. The latter are the people our parents warned us about—the people we cross to the other side of the street to avoid. They reveal human nature at its most base and basic levels. That's probably why they are so interesting to read about.

The Montana Historical Society presented its first "Speaking Ill of the Dead: Jerks in Montana History" session at its annual Montana History Conference in 1989. The session was the brainchild of Dave Walter, then the society's reference librarian and resident walking encyclopedia of Montana's history. Like many of us, Dave had grown weary of the excessive tributes to Montana's founding fathers that proliferated during the state's centennial year. The effusive praise had become a little tiresome, and it was not good history.

For instance, in the rush to commemorate our state's entry into the union, Montanans sang the praises of copper king William A. Clark, banker and railroad financier Sam Hauser, Wilbur Fisk Sanders, and the like. Their fans had conveniently forgotten or overlooked that all of these men had less than sterling sides as well.

In 1899 Clark openly and unremorsefully bribed his way into the U.S. Senate, which promptly censured him for it. Clark was an embarrassment to a group not exactly known for its high moral character at that time. Hauser misused the money deposited in his bank by trusting Helenans, who ultimately suffered for it during the Panic of 1893. Sanders, the Vigilante Lawyer, and his radical Republican cronies falsely accused Territorial Secretary Thomas Francis Meagher of all kinds of heinous activities during his brief career in Montana in the mid-1860s. Sanders's campaign was so successful that it continues to besmirch Meagher's reputation well into the twenty-first century.

Even Montana's finest had their dark sides. So why not recognize some of the state's admittedly less than perfect citizens? That was the idea behind the "Jerks in Montana History" sessions (and this volume). This collection includes fourteen stories about individuals, groups, and organizations that left the world a better place . . . not through their selfless actions, but rather because they left! They are excellent examples of the worst kind of human behavior—both intentional and unintentional. Some, like Boone Helm, John X. Beidler, and Long George Francis, relished their work and poor reputations. Others were part victim, part villain, using gender or circumstance to justify their actions, but who would not consider their behavior reprehensible. Others were just plain bad and did not care what anyone thought.

Perhaps some of the allure of "jerks" is that few of us really fall into that category. We can thus be entertained by the antics of reprehensible people who do things we would never seriously consider doing ourselves. Or maybe, as the recent emergence of "reality TV" indicates, there is a little bit of the jerk in all of us, and watching other people act outrageously is somehow cathartic. In any case, the "Jerks in Montana History" session at the Montana History Conference continues to be popular, drawing a packed house every year.

This collection also owes a lot to Dorothy Johnson and Professor R. T. Turner's 1973 homage to the Obnoxious, the *Bedside Book of Bastards.* They set the standard for the presentation of unpleasant subjects by injecting humor into the short biographies of such loathsome folk as Lucius Cornelius Sulla, the Borgias, and Ivan the Terrible. The book's subtitle puts that book, and this one, in the proper perspective: *A Rich Collection of Counterirritants to the Exasperations of Contemporary Life.*

History demonstrates that amorality and impulse can, for some people, govern their actions toward whatever or whoever bothers them. Sometimes that behavior comes with a price tag—including the possibility of being roasted at the annual Montana History Conference.

This volume is not about one-dimensional villains but rather multifaceted people reacting to trying times. People are products of their times and react to adversity according to existing cultural norms. However, most of the people in this book went above and beyond the dictates of those norms. Their poor behavior transcends time, much as the behavior of George Washington, Abraham Lincoln, and Theodore Roosevelt transcends time in a more positive sense.

So, dear reader, whether you enjoy this volume as good history, good stories, or both, just be thankful that you won't be included in future volumes of this series!

Foil for the Good Guys: Toussaint Charbonneau
Kristin L. Gallas

Wanted: French-Canadian fur trader looking for adventure. Bilingual. Hunting and boatman skills a plus. Good cooking appreciated. Shoshone wife a must.

Fort Mandan *Gazette*, 1804

IT IS EASY TO IMAGINE THAT TOUSSAINT CHARBONNEAU MIGHT HAVE answered an ad something like this, padding his résumé like any self-respecting job candidate hoping to rise in the ranks and garner a pay raise.

From humble beginnings, Toussaint Charbonneau passed through life with the uncanny knack of being at the right place at the right time. He stumbled in and out of history with enough dumb luck to manage to survive the catastrophes that life tossed at him. Today, other than the journals of Meriwether Lewis and William Clark, little reliable information is available about Charbonneau. The journals show a man who was not equipped for life on the frontier, let alone as part of a major military and scientific expedition.

Born in the vicinity of Montreal, Canada, about 1759, Toussaint led an "itinerant life during his apprenticeship in the fur trade, shuttling from one post to another on the Canadian frontier." Although minimal documentation exists for his formative years, records do indicate that he worked as an engagé, or common laborer, for the North West Company between 1793 and 1796. In May 1795, fur trader John MacDonell reported that an old Saultier woman stabbed Charbonneau with a large awl at the Manitou-a-banc end of the Portage la Prairie while he was raping one of her daughters. Still smarting from his humiliating wound, the thirty-six-year-old Charbonneau left the North West Company and later appeared at Metaharta Village on the Knife River in present North Dakota, where he set himself up as an independent agent trading among the Mandan and Hidatsa tribes.

While with the Mandan, Charbonneau developed a friendship

with fellow interpreter Rene Jesseaume. The men were perfect for each other. Both enhanced their already questionable reputations by, among other things, prostituting their wives when in need of extra cash.

In the spring of 1833 Prince Maximilian of Wied recorded in his journal that Charbonneau was known by five names within the Mandan-Hidatsa villages: "Chief of the little village," "the man who possesses many gourds," "the great horse from abroad," "the forest bear," and a fifth that "is not very refined"—hence not given. So vile and sexually explicit was this name that the prince's delicate sensibilities wouldn't allow him to repeat it.

It is here in the Mandan-Hidatsa villages, sometime between 1800 and 1803, that Charbonneau purchased and married two recently captured Shoshone women, including the thirteen-year-old Sacagawea. Though barely into her teens, she would play an important role in the Lewis and Clark Expedition, overshadowing her husband in the annals of history.

Charbonneau lived well in Metaharta with his Indian wives and the benefits of his successful fur trapping. Then along came two Americans leading a rugged bunch of men up the Missouri, with the intent of going to the Pacific Ocean. They needed assistance from the locals for the journey. During the winter of 1804–1805, while Lewis and Clark were holed up at Fort Mandan, Charbonneau courted them for a spot in the expedition. He cozied up to the captains and promoted himself as an all-purpose outdoorsman and highly skilled interpreter.

Historians have long noted that the most decisive factor in Charbonneau's hire was his Shoshone wife Sacagawea, whose tribe Lewis and Clark hoped to meet on their journey westward. The reality was that the captains wanted just her; Charbonneau came along as part of the package. Along for the ride was their infant son, Jean Baptiste, also known as "Pomp," who was born February 11, 1805. Historian Gordon Speck later wrote:

> If millions of words have been written about the leaders of the expedition, only a few less have been printed about Sacagawea, the bird woman. But few of her admirers could name her husband. In fact there is almost a legend that she was a frontier Madonna without husband or other earthly attributes.

Detail of Sacagawea and Toussaint Charbonneau from
Lewis and Clark at Three Forks by Edgar S. Paxson, Oil on
Canvas, 1912, Mural in the Montana State Capitol.
MONTANA HISTORICAL SOCIETY, HELENA.
DON BEATTY, PHOTOGRAPHER.

While the Corps was awaiting their spring departure, Charbonneau visited his former North West Company employer at its trading
post in Gros Ventres country. He returned with stories of lavish cele-
brations, lengths of gay cloth, fancy garments, 200 rounds of ammuni-
tion, and almost 10 feet of tobacco. So annoyed was Clark with
Charbonneau that he accused the man of taking a bribe from the
Nor'Westers. This only added to the ill will between the captains and
Charbonneau, which peaked with Charbonneau's demand to be
excused from all guard duty and common labor. Charbonneau also
insisted that he be allowed to trade privately while on the expedition.
Of course the captains did not acquiesce, and Charbonneau quit the
expedition. A week later, however, he asked the captains to take him

back. Why Charbonneau returned to the captains' employ is unknown, but speculation is that he very much wanted to go to the Pacific and be paid to trade privately with other Indian tribes.

The Corps of Discovery, including the Charbonneau family, set off from Fort Mandan on April 7, 1805, en route to the Pacific Ocean. Much maligned and misunderstood, the actions of Charbonneau during the expedition are numerous and entertaining. The captains frequently mentioned him in their journals—mostly because of his ineptness and the danger he presented to the mission. Historian Gordon Speck observes that, "a close reading of the expedition journals will quickly disclose that Charbonneau was very often given tasks for which he had no ability with nearly disastrous effects. . . ." Incredibly, Charbonneau, a man who had supposedly lived in the wilderness for many years, was unable to perform rudimentary frontier tasks. He couldn't hunt, swim, or steer a canoe. He exhibited the same incompetence that characterized his experience as a member of the Corps throughout his life.

On May 14, just a month after leaving Fort Mandan, Charbonneau committed a serious blunder that nearly resulted in the death of Corps members. While he was steering one of the pirogues on the Missouri River, a short distance past the mouth of the Milk River, a sudden gust of wind struck the craft's sail and caused it to list and take on water. Lewis reported that

> Charbono [sic] cannot swim and is perhaps the most timid waterman in the world . . . Charbono still crying to his god for mercy, had not yet recollected the rudder, nor could the repeated orders of the Bowsman, Cruzat [sic], bring him to his recollection until he threatened to shoot him instantly if he did not take hold of the rudder and do his duty . . .

Clark noted in his journal that Sacagawea's presence and level head were the saving grace in the incident. She caught all the articles that floated out of the pirogue, including papers, instruments, and nearly all their trade goods. Not for the last time, Charbonneau's swift and steady wife upstaged him. Clark noted that on many days Charbonneau and Sacagawea walked on the shore rather than ride in the boats. Charbonneau's lack of swimming ability, fear of drowning, and propensity to panic made him unable to function rationally in crisis situations.

Charbonneau's weapon of choice was a knife, although on the "wild frontier" it seems that a knife would be of little assistance when hunting for food or defending oneself from a wild animal, like a grizzly bear. It just so happened that Charbonneau encountered a "white bear" while out with George Drouillard, one of the expedition's most competent frontiersmen. Even though shimmying up a tree and hiding were considered acceptable defenses against grizzlies, Charbonneau—who was in possession of a gun—decided to run and hide in a thicket, leaving the task of killing the bear to Drouillard. A poor shot under the best of circumstances, Charbonneau would probably have missed the bear anyway.

Jealousy was also apparently one of Charbonneau's weaknesses. Camped near the village of Sacagawea's brother Cameahwait, on the night of August 14, 1805, both Captains Lewis and Clark recorded an incident of domestic violence in camp. Lewis wrote, ". . . this evening Charbonneau struck his Indian woman for which Captain Clark gave him a severe reprimand." Clark noted, "I checked our interpreter for striking his woman at their dinner." Charbonneau's character suggests that he may have felt more than a little jealousy about his wife's new-found importance to the expedition and retaliated the best way he knew how. There is no record of Sacagawea's reaction to the incident.

As ineffectual as Charbonneau seemed to be as a frontiersman, he possessed two qualities that redeemed him in the eyes of the captains. Although he spoke very little English, he was conversant in Hidatsa and French. During a meeting with the Salish, as recounted by Clark, "I spoke . . . to Labieche in English—he translated to Charbonneau in French—he to his wife in Minnetaree (Hidatsa)—she in Shoshone to the [Shoshone Indian] boy—the boy in Tushepaw to that nation."

Lewis was most impressed by "what our right hand cook, Charbonneau, calls the boudin blanc, or white pudding." A frontier delicacy made of buffalo gut and entrails, this coarse sausage dish was a treat for the Corps. Lewis lamented in his journal, ". . . the Indians have informed us that we should shortly leave the buffalo [country] . . . and at all events the white puddings will be irretrievably lost and Charbonneau [will be] out of employment."

Charbonneau's culinary skills seemed only to extend as far as sausage making, as he nearly killed his wife with food. While caching at the Great Falls, Clark recorded: "Sacagawea . . . ate heartily of the raw white apples, together with a considerable quantity of dried fish. Her fever returned. Capt. Lewis rebuked Charbonneau for allowing her to eat such food, for he previously told him what she should eat." Like a hero, Lewis came to Sacagawea's rescue with "a dose of diluted vitriol, and later thirty drops of laudanum, which gave her a tolerable night's rest."

To put Charbonneau's actions in context, he wasn't the only member of the expedition to do stupid things—although his were more numerous and blatant than the others'. Near the end of the journey, on August 11, 1806, on the Missouri below the mouth of the Yellowstone, Lewis and one-eyed Pierre Cruzatte, the Corps' most able fiddler, separated from the party to hunt elk. Lewis later wrote:

> I was in the act of firing on the Elk a second time when a ball struck my left thye about an inch below my hip joint, missing the bone it passed through the left thye and cut the thickness of the bullet across the hinder part of the right thye; the stroke was very severe; I instantly supposed that Cruzatte had shot me in mistake for an Elk as I was dressed in brown leather and he cannot see very well. . . . Cruzatte seemed much alarmed and declared if he shot me it was not his intention. . . . I do not believe that the fellow did it intentionally but after finding that he had shot me was anxious to conceal his knowledge of having done so. The ball had lodged in my breeches which I knew to be the ball of the short rifles such as that he had.

Practically caught red-handed, Cruzatte never admitted to mistaking Lewis's posterior for an elk.

Clark's slave, York, frequently used his skin color to bed Indian women. Granted, other members of the Corps also engaged in sexual relations with Indian women, so it may be safe to say that in 1806 and 1807 there were many mixed-blood babies born along the path of the expedition. When the men came down with a genital itch, Lewis treated them with mercury—potentially killing them faster with mercury poisoning than the venereal diseases would have.

George Shannon, the best educated of the enlisted men and an expert woodsman, got lost. Thinking he had fallen behind while hunting, he was actually traveling ahead of the boats and remained geographically challenged for more than two weeks before rejoining the expedition.

Even Captain Lewis was not exempt from making bad decisions. He contracted syphilis from an Indian woman and brought along only

120 gallons of whiskey for thirty-three people to last over two years—not to mention the iron-frame boat fiasco! Lewis attributed the malfunction of the boat to the lack of proper gum to seal the seams, but in reality the hides could not have been adequately attached to the iron frame. The failure of the iron-framed monstrosity, which he expected to carry at least four tons, sent Lewis into a severe depression. He ordered his favorite boat be sunk in the river.

Toussaint Charbonneau's misdeeds were undoubtedly the best known in the Corps of Discovery. After the expedition returned to St. Louis in 1806, Lewis forwarded a roster of the expedition members to Secretary of War Henry H. Dearborn. In this document he classified the Corps' members and made remarks on many. About Charbonneau, Lewis wrote, "A man of no particular merit; was useful as an interpreter only. . . ." In retrospect, author Robert Lange offered this: "It is perhaps unfair to expect Charbonneau to perform as a hero simply because he was hired out to a heroic troupe." Charbonneau was the least courageous member of a group that has since been honored with heroic status in American history.

Clark offered to take Jean Baptiste, "Pomp," to St. Louis and raise him in a proper home with an education. The Charbonneaus refused the offer, as Pomp was only nineteen months old. In 1811, at the age of six, Pomp was brought, possibly by Charbonneau, to St. Louis and deposited in Clark's care for proper schooling and to be raised as a respectable young man. When Sacagawea died in March 1813 at Fort Manuel, located on the Missouri River between the Arikara and Mandan villages, Charbonneau was absent from the trading post. Clark believed that Charbonneau was dead and assumed guardianship of Pomp and one-year-old Lisette, Charbonneau and Sacagawea's daughter.

The numerous gaps in Charbonneau's life are to be expected from one who could not read or write. His life after the Lewis and Clark Expedition is cloudy, with only occasional incidences where he momentarily emerges from the darkness. He drifted around the upper Missouri and lower Yellowstone regions, acquiring and discarding wives as he went. He worked for whoever would hire him and offered the best female companionship; he was a brazen man of the flesh who never pretended to respectability.

Charbonneau stumbled back into history in mid-September 1812. He arrived at Fort Manuel shouting that the Indians had just killed Francois Lecompte, another Manuel Lisa employee. John Luttig, the post commander and no fan of Charbonneau, accused the French-

Canadian of cowardice, saying that he had "run off and left the poor fellow. . . ." Charbonneau made no comment against these remarks, and two days later he and his partner in crime, Rene Jesseaume, left for Gros Ventre country to get back some supposedly stolen horses. Post commander Luttig documented his thoughts on the duo's doings:

> Charbonneau and Jesseaume keep us in constant uproar with their histories and wish to make fear among the engagés. These two rascals ought to be hung for their perfidy. They do more harm than good to the American government, stir up the Indians and pretend to be friends to the white people at the same time, but we find them to be our enemies.

After years of wandering through the West, with sometime employment by the U.S. Army or a fur company, Charbonneau returned to the Gros Ventre tribe in October 1834 to find his domestic affairs in an uproar—one of his wives had run away. Who could blame her?

In October 1838, seventy-nine-year-old Charbonneau purchased a fourteen-year-old Assiniboine girl from American Fur Company trader Francis Chardon who noted that it was she "who had 'roused a spring fret in the blood of his many wives. . . .'" After providing a feast in honor of his matrimony, the old fellow went to bed with his young wife "with the intention of doing his best."

As all good things must come to an end, so did Charbonneau's life sometime in 1839. It is not known how he met his end, but it may have been in the arms of a beautiful young woman. From Taos to Kansas, from the Great Salt Lake to Yellowstone and the Pacific Ocean, Charbonneau saw it all. He kept company with U.S. Army captains, European royalty, Indian tribes, and French Canadians alike. A scoundrel to the end, Toussaint Charbonneau was a panderer, boaster, liar, brawler, coward, wife-beater, and wife trader—a foul-minded and pretty much useless bit of frontier scum and an opportunist who had the good fortune of being at the right place at the right time. In many ways he was merely a product of his time, a man whose poor behavior would later characterize many others involved in the fur trade. As the grand fool in a party of competent men, Charbonneau's actions were conspicuously at the top of the Lewis and Clark Expedition's careless deeds. His disproportionate wrongdoings made the others look first-rate—the foil for the good guys.

Sources

A wealth of information exists regarding the Lewis and Clark Expedition, with the journals forming the nucleus (DeVoto, Bernard. *The Journals of Lewis and Clark.* Cambridge, MA: Riverside Press, 1953). There is a major gap in the recorded history of Toussaint Charbonneau; as noted, his lack of writing ability accounts for some of that. Contemporary sources that document his life turn up amusing anecdotes of an itinerant life, including Prince Maximilian of Wied's journal (Thwaites, Ruben Gold. *Early Western Travels 1748–1846.* Cleveland, OH: Arthur H. Clark, 1907) and the records of Manual Lisa employee John Luttig (Speck, Gordon. *Breeds and Half Breeds.* New York: Clarkson N. Potter, Inc, 1969).

Many secondary sources already exist, musing on the life and times of Charbonneau and Sacagawea: Robert E. Lange, "Poor Charbonneau! Was He as Incompetent as the Journals/Narratives Make Him Out to Be?" *We Proceeded On,* Vol. 6, #2 (May 1980) 14–17; Irving W. Anderson, "Profiles of the American West: A Charbonneau Family Portrait," *The American West: Magazine of Western History,* Vol. 17, #2 (March/April 1980) 4–13, 58–64; Dennis R. Ottoson, "Toussaint Charbonneau, a Most Durable Man," *South Dakota History,* Vol. 6 (1976) 152–185; and LeRoy R. Hafen, ed. *The Mountain Men and the Fur Trade* (Glendale, CA: The Arthur H. Clark Company, 1972).

Simon Pepin: Reprehensible "Father of Havre"

Dave Walter

WILLIAM ANDREWS CLARK AND MARCUS DALY SO DOMINATE THE POPULAR economic history of Montana that one is hard pressed to see beyond their backlit silhouettes. The eminence of these late-nineteenth-century "Copper Kings" derives primarily from their ability to direct commercial enterprises that extended far beyond mining operations to their involvement in national and international finance, real estate, transportation, lumber, public relations, and politics.

This Clark-Daly dominance detracts from another category of Montana's generally unrecognized capitalists arrayed in the shadows. Like the Copper Kings, these second-echelon entrepreneurs operated from about 1875 to 1920, as Montana evolved from a territory into a state and became industrialized. Ultimately these unheralded men proved to be more crucial to the survival of many of Montana's communities than was either Clark or Daly.

These second-tier entrepreneurs directed smaller, but also multi-faceted, commercial empires and had a significant effect on their area's economic fortunes. On a local level, these pioneer businessmen are now identified as founding fathers and pillars of the community. But at the time they were simply called capitalists.

Most small Montana communities boast at least one of these entrepreneurs; larger towns and cities can trace their early development to two or three of them: men like Andrew B. Hammond of Missoula, Herbert O. Cowan of Great Falls, Albert L. Babcock of Billings, Arthur W. Miles of Livingston, Charles E. Conrad of Kalispell, and Henry F. Douglas of Glendive.

These men were not out-of-state opportunists who deserted in the face of a depression or depletion of a resource. They were immigrants to Montana Territory who arrived with neither fanfare nor backing. What they did possess was vision, an unwavering work ethic, and an intense determination to succeed in a frontier economy.

They created, practically from nothing, a small empire of enterprises that was personally rewarding.

Moreover, they helped to promote their communities and provided leadership and economic stability—despite natural and financial disasters. Their commitment to their communities was constant and pervasive and extended far beyond the world of finance. They were also involved in the social, humanitarian, and political lives of their towns. A century before "Build Montana" became a slogan, these men *were* building Montana.

The lives, the commercial enterprises, the community development—even the Victorian residences—of these entrepreneurs bespoke their faith in their settlements' stability and future. Ultimately these area-oriented capitalists, who have been generally ignored by Montana historians, epitomize community development in the state. These men began conservatively in Montana Territory's fiscal wilderness, worked diligently, perceived changing economic patterns, diversified their operations, and became the financial cornerstones of their communities.

One such man was Simon Pepin. Generally uncelebrated, this Havre entrepreneur exemplifies economic leadership in small-town Montana. His sphere of influence was areawide, rather than statewide, but his commercial activities were crucial to the initial and continued progress of his Hi-Line community. The November 16, 1914, *Havre Daily Reporter* called Pepin "the man who, more than any other, was the father of this city."

However, a closer look at Simon's life reveals some black stripes. Indeed, Simon Pepin was a "zebra"—a Montana character who mixed admirable and reprehensible characteristics inside the same skin. But before we delve into his seamy side—which qualifies him as a jerk—we should establish his white stripes, his generally admirable characteristics.

Simon Pepin was born on December 20, 1840, to a large French-Canadian Catholic family in St. Michel, Quebec. His mother, Marie Peprino, died when Simon was four years old. At the age of fifteen, he left the family farm and moved to the United States. He worked in a brickyard in Saco, Maine, until the outbreak of the Civil War. Then he headed west and worked on steamboats on the Missouri and upper Mississippi Rivers.

In 1863, at the age of twenty-three, Simon traveled to Utah and ended up in Virginia City, Idaho Territory. The next year he was employed as a teamster by Charles A. Broadwater and the Diamond R Freighting Company.

Simon Pepin, 1913.

Although he braved the Corinne-Montana road in all seasons and under extreme weather conditions, Simon never failed to deliver his cargo intact, usually well before the contracted date. Because of his limited education, he kept the financial details of the shipments in his head. The quiet, stocky teamster was likable, well mannered, and exceedingly thrifty, and his keen business sense was admired and exploited by his employers.

During the 1860s and 1870s, Simon worked very hard, saved his money, and built a reputation for reliability. On his own, he bought and sold cattle to Indian agencies and military forts, both stable markets. By the mid-1880s he was running 20,000 cattle and 2,500 horses north of the Milk River, under the P Cross brand.

Simon also had become involved in the construction of Fort Assinniboine in the late 1870s. With Edward T. Broadwater, cousin of Charles, he freighted supplies to the fort, managed the post store, and filled beef contracts for the U.S. Army. "Pepin's Camp" on Beaver Creek rapidly became the center for the fort's civilian activity, much of which catered to the isolated soldiers' needs and desires.

Few men in 1882 could perceive how northern Montana would change within a decade. But Simon's experience in steamboat and wagon train transportation, as well as his understanding of the Native American–military situation, dictated his next moves. He began to purchase the homestead lands of several relatives who had filed claims north of the Milk River and in the bottoms of Bull Hook Creek, several miles east of Fort Assinniboine.

In this heyday of the open range, Simon acquired title to key water-hole and creek-bottom properties that were held by his relatives. By the mid-1880s he owned 5,000 acres in the area, particularly in Bull Hook Bottoms, along with water sources north of the Milk River and south toward the Bear's Paw Mountains. When the Great Northern steamed across the Hi-Line in autumn 1887, Simon Pepin was already well established.

In 1890, as James J. Hill determined to push the Great Northern's mainline west over Marias Pass to Puget Sound, Hill decided to relocate his division point to the area's best water supply. Not surprisingly, Ed Broadwater and Simon Pepin owned this land in Bull Hook Bottoms, about 7 miles east of Assiniboine Station.

The men struck a deal with Hill. Broadwater and Pepin would donate forty acres apiece for a government townsite to be platted in the Bottoms. Hill, in return, would move the division-point shops and roundhouse in from Assinniboine Station. In this way, Simon assured the long-term economic stability of the settlement that would soon be named Havre. He benefited directly from the deal and legitimately can be called "the father of Havre."

In 1891 Simon moved from Fort Assinniboine to Havre with Ed Broadwater. The pair established what would become one of the largest general-merchandise businesses in northern Montana: the Broadwater-Pepin Mercantile Company. The partners also built the large Broadwater-Pepin building, which came to symbolize Havre's economic promise.

At the same time, Simon continued to develop his livestock holdings and purchased additional blocks of land in what would become Cascade and Hill Counties. With Broadwater he also became involved in Havre banking and real estate–development operations.

In 1890, at Fort Assinniboine, Simon had married LaRose Trottier, a Cree woman with three children (at least one of whom most likely was fathered by Simon). In December 1891 the couple had a daughter, Elizabeth, and in 1892 the family moved into a log house in Havre. By the next winter, Simon had constructed a modest five-room brick-and-frame home on the corner of Fourth Avenue and Third Street.

During the 1890s Simon rebuilt this house into a fourteen-room mansion that featured a French-style tower and roofline. He encircled the entire block with an elaborate wrought-iron fence. This successful capitalist had created a residence that confirmed his faith in the community's future—and his own place in it.

Simon Pepin became a wealthy man through unrelenting labor and insightful business decisions. He became a community builder. After Havre's devastating downtown fire of 1904, he immediately announced his plans to rebuild the mercantile—in brick! He also floated low-interest loans to other businessmen who would rebuild quickly.

Simon donated acreage for the first Catholic cemetery in Havre. He gave land for the first Catholic church, and he substantially funded the construction of the second Catholic church. He made a large cash donation toward the building of Sacred Heart Hospital. He also provided a sizable chunk of land for Pepin Park. Dozens of local ranchers and businessmen survived periods of hardship with the assistance of small personal loans negotiated in Simon's drawing room.

Simon Pepin died in 1914, at the age of seventy-three, leaving an estate of more than $1 million. The November 14, 1914, *Hill County Democrat* eulogized:

"In the demise of Mr. Pepin, Havre loses a booster, a pioneer, a

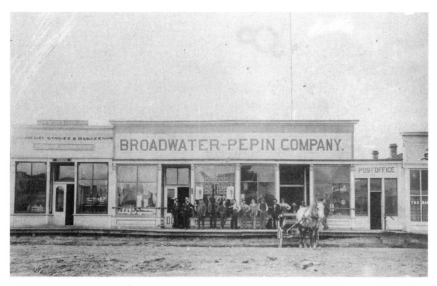

Broadwater-Pepin Company between Second and
Third Avenues on First Street, Havre, 1894.
MONTANA HISTORICAL SOCIETY, HELENA.

torch-bearer, and a good friend. His loss is immeasurable.

"Simon Pepin was admired and loved by all. He never catered to caste and cared naught for society's deceitful smile. He adored industry and always looked for character in the man.

"His life was a complete success, and he always came honestly by his personally earned wealth. . . . He took great pride in the beloved city of Havre. He generated and enjoyed its rapid growth from a little shack-town to a great city. . . .

"Those who knew him best, admired him most."

Simon's life in Montana from 1863 to 1914 is representative of that group of second-echelon entrepreneurs whom historians of Montana have ignored. Not as monumental as a Clark and not as spectacular as a Daly, these pioneer capitalists nevertheless built spheres of influence by combining transportation, mercantile, lumber, mining, livestock, banking, and real-estate enterprises. In the course of amassing personal fortunes, these men created a sound economic base on which their communities relied. They invested in their settlements and their institutions with an unwavering commitment.

Simon Pepin fits this profile with remarkable accuracy. So what is questionable about "the Father of Havre?" Where are his black stripes?

One indication is the manner in which Simon amassed more than

9,000 acres of land in Cascade and Hill Counties. These holdings came at a dubious price for Simon's family. In the 1870s and 1880s, Simon brought to northern Montana his brothers and sisters, nieces and nephews, and cousins and had them homestead predetermined water-source properties. Simon then purchased these adjacent homestead properties and created two large ranch complexes, one north of the Milk River and the other south of Havre, toward the Bear's Paw Mountains.

There was nothing illegal in these actions. Everyone did it, if he could, and Simon had promised his relatives his economic help if they ever needed it. But when these same relatives later fell on hard times, Simon systematically ignored their pleas for assistance. Once he held title to the properties, his family ties frayed.

Another indication of Simon Pepin's black stripes is revealed in a newspaper account of a speech that he gave to a group of Indians assembled for the Grass Dance festival outside Havre in 1904:

> I came here when the Bear's Paw Mountains were no bigger than gopher mounds. At that time you were a thrifty people, able to play a poker hand with the best of us. For some time I despaired of doing well in this country—so fertile and resourceful were you in the great American game of commerce and trade. Yet I noticed even then that your appetite for firewater was good. I told Ed Broadwater that it would finally defeat you in the race for wealth.
>
> I am glad to see that my prophecy was so fulfilled!
>
> I reasoned that, if you were going to lose your ponies and wigwam comforts and embellishments, you had just as well lose them to Ed and me, as to anyone. So we stayed in the country and shared with you our bacon, while we garnered the harvest you and your sires had tended.
>
> I can't see why you don't go off and work a little. Your indolence is preventing me from getting the money that I need.

However, the real indication of Simon's dark side comes from a hint found in some of the deeds for Simon's more than 500 land transactions: "Simon Pepin, a single man." Is this just legal phraseology? No! Simon Pepin constructed an elaborate legal house of cards to deny his marriage and his paternity!

LaRose Trottier, the Cree woman Simon had married in 1890, never lived in the mansion he built at Third Street and Fourth Avenue in Havre! And indications are that this was by Simon's decree. Rose remained in the log cabin at the back of the lot. Simon supplied Rose's transportation, her food, her clothing, and her other necessities. He ate his suppers in the cabin and spent his nights there until his death. But only the families of Simon's nieces and nephews—and his daughter, Elizabeth—lived in the mansion.

What can explain this peculiar arrangement? Only that Rose was an obvious embarrassment to a highly successful businessman. She was Indian; she spoke only snatches of English; she preferred reservation clothing to store-bought finery. Although the Pepins' arrangement was known to the entire community, Simon legally hid his wife and children. Only Elizabeth became visible in 1902—when Simon legally adopted his own daughter!

Simon's will is a key document in this legal fabrication. In it he bequeathed a pittance of $500 to each niece and nephew. He willed a similarly meager $3,000 to a brother, but made some substantial contributions to Havre institutions. The balance of more than $900,000 fell to Elizabeth. Rose did not receive even the normal one-third "dower share" of the estate. Rather, Simon left the minuscule sum of $5,000 for Rose's care, a fund to be administered by Elizabeth.

Elizabeth at this time (1914) was twenty-three years old and married to Frank Meyers. She immediately and successfully petitioned the Havre district court to commit Rose to the Catholic Home of the Good Shepherd in Helena . . . ostensibly "to dry her out."

Rose was sequestered at the Home of the Good Shepherd for one year and three days, until Simon's will had been probated. Elizabeth then went to Helena and retrieved Rose—but only after Rose promised not to sign any legal papers challenging the probate. During the next ten years (1916–1926), Elizabeth and Frank sold off most of Simon's holdings and moved to St. Paul.

In 1921 Rose married Frank Baker. In 1926 Baker and Havre attorney C. R. Stranahan convinced Rose that she could still obtain her rightful one-third dower share of Simon's estate, and filed legal papers in her behalf.

Rose won the challenge case on the Havre district-court level. In 1927, however, Elizabeth appealed that decision to the Montana Supreme Court. The supreme court reversed the lower court's decision on the basis that the 1890 marriage between Rose and Simon Pepin was not a legal marriage. Therefore Rose could not claim the dower share.

This ruling left Rose destitute and at the mercy of her legal adversary and daughter, Elizabeth. Elizabeth claimed that the $5,000 left by Simon for the care of Rose had long ago been depleted. Thus Simon Pepin's elaborate legal scheme to deny his marriage and paternity proved ultimately successful—as administered by his "adopted" daughter.

Most assuredly Simon Pepin is "the Father of Havre" and a prime example of the second-echelon entrepreneurs who became the "building blocks" of a score of Montana communities. And given Simon's white stripes, you may find the term "reprehensible" too strong for him. But you must agree that, at least, he is a man with broad black stripes as well as white ones.

∿

Sources

See biographical information on Simon Pepin in the following: Hill County Bicentennial Commission, *Grit, Guts and Gusto: A History of Hill County* (Havre: Bear Paw Printers, 1976); Robert C. Lucke, *Historic Homes of North Central Montana* (Havre: Bear Paw Printers, 1977); *Progressive Men of Montana* (Chicago: A. W. Bowen, 1902); Robert Mastrandrea, "Research Paper on Simon Pepin, 1840–1914," Northern Montana College, n.d.; "Simon Pepin Has Given the City of Havre a Site for a Beautiful Park," *Havre Plaindealer,* November 21, 1908; "Old Simon Pepin Home, Landmark Being Removed," *Havre Daily News,* June 12, 1951; "Simon Pepin Can Justly Be Called 'the Father of Havre,'" (Havre) *Hi-Line Herald,* August 15, 1963.

The Work Projects Administration, Writer's Project "Livestock History of Montana" (Montana Historical Society Library Microfilm #250) contains pertinent short pieces entitled "Pepin and Broadwater," "L. K. Devlin," "Early Events of Hill County," "The Story of [Simon] Pepin," "Orator [Simon] Pepin," and "The P-Cross Cattle Company." See also two pieces from the *Montana Newspaper Association Inserts* series: "Squaw of Pepin Will Get Dower," October 11, 1926, and "Diamond R, State's Biggest Freight Outfit, Was Started to Save Money, Not Make It," January 18, 1937.

Simon Pepin can be tracked in the R. L. Polk directories for Havre and Chouteau/Hill Counties. See also *Manuscript Collection 99: Broadwater-Pepin Company Records,* 1899–1931, Montana Historical Society Archives, Helena, Montana.

The activities of Pepin and his relatives can be investigated further in the series of Havre newspapers: the *Havre Advertiser,* 1893–1895; the *Havre Plaindealer,* 1902–1921; the *Havre Herald,* 1904–1908; the (Havre) *Hill County Democrat,* 1912–1921, 1923–1929; the *Havre Daily Promoter,* 1916–1918, 1920–1923, 1923–1925; and the *Havre Daily News-Promoter,* 1925–1928.

Haymarket Square: Anatomy of a Lynching

Angie Gifford and Dave Walter

We, the jury, . . . find that James E. Brady came to his death at a place called the Haymarket, in Helena, Lewis and Clark County, Montana, on the morning of October 2, 1901, between 1:30 and 2:00 o'clock, at the hands of unknown parties.

> County Coroner's Jury, October 2, 1901

Mention Helena's vigilantes, and one assumes a story from the 1860s or 1870s. However, there was one "Queen City" lynching that Helenans do not talk about with flamboyant Old West pride. It occurred in the twentieth century—in the very year that Montanans were building a new capitol and at the very time that Helenans were touting their newfound culture and sophistication.

The hanging of James Edward Brady by a vigilante mob early on Wednesday morning, October 2, 1901, strikes a black mark across Helena's historical record. It was a lynching, pure and simple—however much the miscreant deserved it!

Fifty-year-old James Edward Brady's first real brush with the law occurred in the 1880s. Convicted of horse theft, he served five years in the Territorial Prison at Deer Lodge under the name "A. J. Lilly." He returned to the prison in 1897, convicted of forgery, using the name "Henry Grady." Upon his pardon in 1898, Brady located in Whitehall and then in Boulder, where he worked as a section boss for the Northern Pacific Railroad and as a bricklayer. A Boulder jury acquitted the widower Brady of stealing a horse and buggy. Jefferson County authorities, however, suspected Brady of being a pedophile because four young girls told stories of how he had enticed them to his cabin with candy. Local residents acted summarily: They ran the degenerate out of town!

Brady landed in Mitchell, the Great Northern/Montana Central Railway station 17 miles north of Helena (near the current Sieben exit off Interstate 15). Here he worked as a section foreman for the railroad, although he also spent a good deal of time in Helena. In September

1901 a man fitting Brady's description was accused of stealing a horse and buggy at Helena's Central Park and trying to sell it in East Helena. A warrant was issued for the arrest of this man.

On Sunday evening, September 29, Brady caught a freight train from Mitchell into Helena and began a night of drinking in the saloons along Main Street/Last Chance Gulch. At one point he engaged in a bar fight with two soldiers from Fort Harrison and suffered one cut on his ear and another on his nose. Upon running into Deputy Sheriff William McGahan on the street, Brady displayed his wounds and demanded that the lawman arrest the two soldiers. McGahan ignored the request, and Brady continued his binge.

Wherever Brady slept that night, he was back to barhopping by early morning. At about 9:50 A.M. he encountered a young girl playing on the north lawn of the Lewis and Clark County Courthouse and struck up a conversation with her.

Hazel Price (this surname has been changed in deference to the family) was almost six years old and an afternoon-kindergarten student at Central School. An only child, she lived with her mother and grandmother in the Big Anne Flats at 16 North Rodney, directly behind the county jail. Hazel had become a favorite in the "courthouse district" because of her bright, cheerful manner. She often played around the courthouse and the jail with her best friend, the six-year-old daughter of Lewis and Clark County Sheriff Jeff O'Connell.

Hazel's parents—Peter and Gertrude Price—recently had separated. Peter Price had moved to Butte and found a job with the Reed Cab and Transfer Company, working as a transfer agent at the city's railroad depots. While Gertrude Price clerked at Mrs. O. N. Gill's Millinery Shop in Last Chance Gulch, Esther Greening (this surname likewise has been changed) looked after her granddaughter. Neither woman believed that Hazel was at any risk playing in the neighborhood.

James Edward Brady enticed little Hazel Price away from the courthouse lawn with the promise of a streetcar ride to the Broadwater Natatorium, west of the city. As the pair walked down the alley beside the county jail, they encountered an unsuspecting neighbor lady, who exchanged pleasantries with Hazel. By 10:10 A.M. the two had reached the streetcar barns near the intersection of South Main and Cutler.

When Brady learned that the next car to the Broadwater did not depart for forty-five minutes, he asked the destination of the car then preparing to leave. When he was told "East Helena," he bought tickets for himself and Hazel. The pair rode the car out Boulder Avenue for 3

Sketch of Hazel Price.
ANACONDA STANDARD, OCTOBER 4, 1901.

miles and disembarked at the stop for the Peck Concentrator, about halfway to East Helena.

Conductor Hugh Gaw saw Brady lead the little girl into an abandoned shack beside the tracks. On the streetcar's return run to Helena, Brady appeared at the door of the shack and waived Gaw's motorman on. It was approximately 10:40 A.M.

The streetcar crews changed at noon, so a new conductor had taken the controls when Brady and Hazel returned to Helena about 12:40 P.M. Brady walked the girl from the streetcar barns up onto Catholic Hill, within 2 blocks of her home. He released her, admonishing her not to say anything to her mother.

In the meantime, Gertrude Price had returned for lunch from the dressmaking shop on Main Street. When she and Grandmother Greening could not locate Hazel in the neighborhood, the young mother contacted Deputy Sheriff McGahan. Together the two searched the courthouse district and the area around Central School for the missing child, but to no avail.

Gertrude's anxiety rapidly was approaching hysteria when Hazel finally appeared at the flat about 1:15 P.M. Sobbing, the little girl told her mother all the sickening, gruesome details of the abduction and sexual assault. Grandmother Greening called Doctors Charles Perrin and Charles Miller, who arrived and administered aid to both mother and daughter. They found Hazel bruised, in shock, and close to collapse. Mrs. Price was frantic and in need of sedation as much as her child.

Deputy McGahan listened to Hazel's story. When she described her assailant—complete with the cuts on his ear and nose—the lawman knew he had a solid lead. After reporting his suspicions to Sheriff O'Connell, McGahan walked down to the streetcar barns to interview Conductor Hugh Gaw. Gaw and his motorman were leaving on the Broadwater run, so the deputy hopped on the trolley as it rolled north along Main Street.

As the two men talked, Gaw looked over to the sidewalk in front of the New York Store. He pointed to a short, heavyset, balding man walking with two companions and said, "There's the man now." McGahan immediately alighted, made for his man, laid a hand on the suspect's shoulder, and said, "I want you!" Both Conductor Gaw and his motorman positively identified Brady as the man who had ridden with a young girl toward East Helena that morning.

By 3:45 P.M., Deputy McGahan's quick work had led to the apprehension of Brady. At the sheriff's office, the suspect identified himself only as "James Edwards" and professed his innocence of any crime. At Sheriff O'Connell's orders, two deputies then led Brady to the Price flat on Rodney Street. Attended by Dr. Perrin, a distraught Hazel was brought into the parlor.

The *Helena Daily Independent* reported: "At the sight of the fellow, little Hazel screamed at the top of her voice. She knew him in an instant and begged, in a most pitiful manner, for the officer to take him away."

While clerks prepared an arrest warrant, the deputies canvassed the Prices' neighbors. One officer interviewed a woman who said that she had seen Hazel with a man that morning in the alley behind the jail. When the woman stood outside Brady's cell, she identified him positively as the person she had encountered that morning.

News of the dastardly Brady assault spread rapidly that evening through the saloons, cigar stores, cafes, and pool halls on Main Street. Some irate Helenans spoke openly about taking the law into their own hands to even the score with Brady. Others decried a judicial system that did not provide a death sentence for criminal assault. By about 11:00 P.M., a group of drinkers in Patrick Duffy's Office Saloon (403 North Main) devised a solution.

The crowd of twenty-five angry, inebriated men pushed up the hill to the county jail and rang the call bell. They demanded the release of Brady to their custody for hanging. Night jailer George Mahrt honestly replied that Brady had been removed from the jail for safekeeping.

In fact, Sheriff O'Connell had anticipated just such a threat. Shortly after 7:00 P.M., he had locked a ball-and-chain ankle cuff on Brady and quietly taken him out the jail's back door into a closed carriage. The two would spend the night at a cabin on Ten Mile Creek in the Helena Valley. Brady slept soundly; O'Connell dozed only fitfully. The sheriff escorted his prisoner back to the jail before 6:00 A.M. on Tuesday.

Peter Price, Hazel's father, had been informed of the assault, and he arrived from Butte on the midnight Montana Central run. He joined his estranged wife's two brothers—George and Alman Greening—at the Office Saloon.

On Tuesday the sheriff feared driving Brady through Helena's streets, so he summoned Justice of the Peace Terrence O'Donnell to the courthouse. For safety, O'Donnell held Brady's arraignment hearing in the sheriff's office. The prisoner waived his preliminary hearing, so bond was fixed at $1,000, awaiting formal charges. During the day, County Attorney Odell W. McConnell interviewed witnesses and drew up those charges.

All three of Helena's daily newspapers—the *Helena Independent* (morning), the *Helena Herald* (evening), and the *Helena Record* (evening)—carried front-page stories on Tuesday. By suppertime the entire community knew of Brady's alleged crime.

Quiet threats against the ex-convict surfaced through the evening in bars along the Gulch, with the strongest words emanating from Duffy's Office Saloon. Still, it remained just talk. An exhausted Sheriff O'Connell finally went to bed about 10:30 P.M. in his second-floor apartment within the jail building. The *Independent* reflected:

"Intimations that there was something brewing were given out early in the evening, but there was . . . no cursing of the prisoner, as there had been the night before. . . . [Most authorities] thought that public feeling had abated somewhat and that the law would be allowed to take its course. The only thing to cause any suspicion whatever was that at midnight there were many men on the streets—men who are in the habit of retiring early."

At about 1:00 A.M., a group of thirty-five men quietly gathered on the southwest corner of Main and Lawrence Streets, beside Haymarket Square. They conferred for a few minutes, were joined by other cells of two and three men each, and finally broke up to march south on Main Street. Observers saw some of the dark figures at the head of the procession carrying sledgehammers, crowbars, axes, and ropes—although no firearms were apparent.

A bystander commented: "One notable feature of the affair was the personnel of the mob. They were not the hobo or bum element of the city at all. They were mostly young, well-dressed. . . . there wasn't any county-jake [sic] business about those fellows. Did you notice them? They all had on fine overcoats and were swell-dressed young fellows."

The number of marchers now had grown to about seventy-five men. Others joined the procession as it climbed Seventh Avenue, passed the Auditorium, and crossed Warren. When the leaders reached the Ewing intersection, they stopped to pull bandanas from their coats, fashioning them into masks for their faces.

Then, again up Ewing the mob surged until it spilled into a pool in front of the main entrance of the jail. The leader and his three captains mounted the rock steps, and one pushed the electric call bell in the massive oak-and-steel doors, reinforced with steel studs and heavy metal straps.

When no one answered the bell, the leader called up a masked man with a large sledge, who began to beat on the formidable double doors in the hope of springing the bolt. After several minutes, this tactic looked futile, so axes were tried, as were pry bars. Finally an exceptionally large fellow pushed through the crowd.

"Let me have that hammer," he said. The man who spoke was masked, but he made everyone feel that something now would happen. The first blow he dealt the door seemed to have effect. The door sprung, and a stream of light shone through for an instant. Blow after blow was dealt, and it was apparent that the door would not last much longer—and it did not.

With the main doors forced, shrouded men poured into the vestibule—only to be faced with their next obstacles: a lighter wooden door, bolted from the inside, and a two-part steel-gate door made of one-inch bars. The leader called through the barriers for night jailer George Mahrt.

Lawrence Street, Haymarket Square between Main and Fuller, Helena, ca. 1898.
MONTANA HISTORICAL SOCIETY, HELENA.

Mahrt had served in this position since early 1899, but he had never been this frightened in his life. About 1:15 A.M., Glenn Foster, a reporter for the *Independent*, had yelled through the jail office's barred window to tell Mahrt that a mob was coming toward the jail from the Gulch. All alone in the office, Mahrt reset the heavy bolt on the outer oak-and-steel doors, checked the locks on the two inner doors, and then tested the three metal-bar doors between the office and the prisoner Brady. By this time the attackers were battering the front doors.

When the mob reached the vestibule, Mahrt heard his name called. He reached through the steel-gate door and unlocked the outer, wooden door so that he could reason with the leaders. Instead, he immediately faced two loaded, cocked pistols—and threats to shoot him if he did not unlock the steel-gate door to the office. At this point, Mahrt concluded that he would give up Brady to save himself and the four other prisoners. He opened the metal-bar door, and the masked men pushed into the office.

"What do you want?" Mahrt asked.

"We want Brady, the fellow that raped the little girl," the spokesman demanded. "Take us to his cell."

After the jailer unlocked two intervening metal-bar doors, about thirty of the mob crowded into the cell block and gathered in front of Brady's cell. The prisoner cowered in the corner, without coat, vest, collar, hat, or tie.

"Are you sure that this is the right man?" the leader asked again.

A shaking Mahrt assured him and then unlocked the cell door. Two captains entered, seized the prisoner, placed a light rope around his neck, and led him out—through the core of vigilantes and into the street, where the crowd had now reached about 125 dark figures.

As the squad leaders encircled Brady and began the march back to Haymarket Square—followed by the crowd—the clock in the courthouse tower pealed the half hour. The vigilantes' entire attack on the county jail had taken just fifteen minutes. Only at this point did Mahrt ring the alarm bell in the sheriff's quarters and wake Jeff O'Connell.

As quiet and orderly as when they had ascended the hill, the businesslike masked men retraced their route down Ewing, Seventh, and Main until they reached Lawrence Street. The squad marched Brady to the base of a telegraph pole standing at the northwest corner of the intersection. The time was 1:45 A.M.

The hushed crowd surrounding the pole had reached about 200 men, many of them masked. Their grim demeanor bespoke their intentions and their need for quick and quiet action. Glenn Foster, the *Independent* reporter on the scene, observed (apparently without irony):

"There were some suggestions as to burning the prisoner, and doing other brutal acts, but the crowd did not wish to do anything brutal. Many were of the opinion that hanging was too good for him. But they also believed that the interests of the community demanded that the affair should come off as quietly as possible and that no brutal actions be permitted."

A dazed Brady pleaded again that he was innocent. The mob's masked spokesman then ordered one of his captains to find Patrick Duffy, the proprietor of the Office Saloon, directly across Main Street from the telegraph pole. Within minutes Duffy appeared and positively identified Brady.

The leader turned to the mob: "Gentlemen, are you satisfied?"

A thunderous "yes" was the reply. At this moment a masked figure forced his way through the crowd to where the prisoner stood. Before anyone could interfere, he struck Brady twice on the face.

"None of that! None of that!" shouted the leader. "Take that man away."

"He's the father of the girl," came the hushed response from those in the crowd who recognized Peter Price, despite his mask.

One of the vigilante captains climbed up the telegraph pole and pitched the noose over the lowest cross-arm. The spokesman ordered Brady's hands tied behind his back and the heavy noose fitted around the prisoner's neck, replacing the lighter hold rope.

"Brady," said the leader, "your time is about up. If you want to offer a prayer, we'll give you a chance now."

The bewildered captive hesitated. "I don't believe that I know how to make a prayer. Won't someone make a prayer for me?" he begged.

For a moment there was perfect silence. Finally a voice in the crowd yelled, "May the Lord forgive you, Brady. That's all I can say to you." Another shouted, "And that's more than he deserves."

An oppressive stillness enveloped the crowd. Then the leader commanded, "Pull away, boys!"

The *Record* reported:

"Instantly those holding the rope rushed about 20 feet ahead, and the wretched man swung back and forth in the air, about 15 feet off the ground. Scarcely a remark was made, but the crowd closely watched their victim.

"He did not move for half a minute, then he drew up his legs two or three times. His body was seen to quiver violently. Then the head fell to one side. There was no further motion, except as the body swung gently in the soft moonlight, making a ghastly picture."

Someone at the base of the pole called out, "Three cheers for the Haymarket boys!" and three hearty cheers rose from the mob.

Again one of the captains climbed the pole. This time he tied the rope's loose end around the victim's feet—thus suspending the body above the onlookers. It was 1:50 A.M., and a crowd of almost 200 had witnessed the extralegal execution. The gathering included most of the Chicago-based touring company from *The Belle of New York,* a comedy that had played at the Helena Theater earlier in the evening. The *Independent* also remarked:

"A noticeable feature of the hanging was the presence of several women who were driven down in a hack a few minutes before the body was drawn upwards."

As scores of other spectators began to arrive at Haymarket Square, the vigilantes removed their masks and blended into the crowd.

Within five minutes, Sheriff O'Connell appeared on the scene, having walked down from the jail. After surveying the situation, he retreated to the Office Saloon and telephoned the county attorney and the county coroner. He then returned to the telegraph pole to protect the crime scene. The lawman remarked to a reporter from the *Record*:

"I did not know a thing about this until it was too late. The night jailer was overpowered by armed men. I don't blame him. There was nothing else for him to do under the circumstances. I was afraid of something like this last night, but I thought the excitement was all over by tonight. This thing is a complete surprise to me. . . . I am awfully sorry that this has happened."

County Coroner Ben C. Brooke finally arrived about 2:35 A.M. He directed an eager bystander to climb the telegraph pole and cut the hangman's rope. Brady's body tumbled with a thud to the base of the pole, and Dr. Brooke pronounced him dead. The coroner and the sheriff loaded the victim's body into a hack and directed the driver to the Herrmann and Company undertaking rooms at 129 Broadway.

As the authorities left the grisly scene, souvenir-seekers slipped in to cut short lengths from a long piece of the hangman's rope, which had been discarded in the street. A reporter for the *Butte Inter Mountain* estimated that about 1,000 people had viewed the body during the forty-five minutes it was suspended from the telegraph pole.

On Wednesday all three Helena dailies ran extensive coverage of the lynching. These extremely detailed accounts revealed that reporters from the papers had accompanied the mob's leaders from the Haymarket, up to the jail, into the cellblock, back down to the Main Street intersection, and during the hanging.

Peter Price caught the Wednesday-noon train back to Butte. In the afternoon, however, County Attorney McConnell issued a warrant for Price's arrest, on the charges of "inciting the lynching" and "complicity in murder."

Some of the morbid curiosity that had pervaded the mostly male crowd on the preceding night spread among Helena's women and children on Wednesday. Lines began forming in front of Herrmann's funeral parlor before 10:00 A.M. By noon, about 950 Helenans—many

Sketch of James Edward Brady.
ANACONDA STANDARD, OCTOBER 6, 1901.

of them youngsters and their mothers—had trooped past the body of James Edward Brady.

Undertakers had neatly tucked the body into a low casket. They again affixed the noose around his neck and coiled the 4-foot lead beside the corpse's head. A few of the most brazen viewers cut short pieces from this rope for souvenirs, until nothing remained but the hangman's noose itself. When County Coroner Brooke encountered this ghoulish scene at 1:00 P.M., he ordered an end to the festivities by locking the funeral parlor doors.

On Wednesday evening, in the Herrmann and Company rooms, Brooke convened a coroner's inquest to determine the parties responsible for Brady's death. Although the official had scheduled the hearing for 8:30 P.M., its beginning was delayed more than an hour. Inexplicably, Alderman Hilary J. Zayas—a member of the coroner's jury—failed to appear until almost 10:00 P.M.

Finally, after County Attorney McConnell established the basic sequence of the mob's actions, he called a series of witnesses to identify the vigilante leaders. However, a pattern quickly developed among the witnesses:

"Yes, I was present at the jail and/or at the hanging."

"No, I did not participate; I was just a spectator."

"No, I was not masked."

"No, I cannot identify any of the vigilantes, because they all were masked."

As a result of this stonewalling tactic, the coroner's jury did not reach a verdict until shortly before midnight. Then it found that Brady "came to his death . . . at the hands of unknown parties."

Reaction among Helena's governmental leaders to this open act of vigilantism was swift and loud. Governor Joseph K. Toole's words, however, were measured:

"Such an outcome I never expected. . . . I had come to believe that so excellent was the administration of Montana's laws that never again would we see in this city a display of mob violence. There is simply no excuse for mob law *anywhere* in Montana. The work of the mob last night, in my opinion, will place the state back many years in the scale of civilization."

The words of District Court Judge Henry Cooper Smith showed no attempt to conceal his outrage. Smith immediately called for a grand-jury investigation of the incident—primarily to identify the vigilantes and to punish them. The judge barely could control his anger as he charged the jury:

> . . . The capital city of the state of Montana has been disgraced by a mob of irresponsible hoodlums and toughs. . . . Brady was murdered by said mob on a public square of this city without trial or proof of guilt. . . .
>
> Lewis and Clark County has a granite and steel jail, which cost approximately $60,000. Between the outside and the cell where Brady was confined are two wooden doors and five steel doors. This jail was constructed from the best modern plans, and yet Brady was taken there from about midnight without breaking a lock or forcing a door. . . .
>
> The killing of Brady was just as much murder as the killing of any other human being without justification or warrant of law. The crime he is supposed to have committed is no excuse for the act of this mob.

Nevertheless, on the streets of Helena rationalizations for the dark-of-night lynching found some sympathy. These arguments decried a Montana law that failed to mandate the death penalty for the sexual assault of a child. Citizens questioned whether the Montana judicial system could mete out just punishment in a timely fashion, even for such a ghastly crime. Critics cited recent cases in which Montana juries—"manipulated by fast-talking lawyers"—had acted with extreme leniency, even after finding the accused guilty.

In the midst of this public controversy on Thursday, two county workers buried Brady's remains. Without any service, they deposited them in "potter's field," near Forestvale Cemetery. That evening Deputy Sheriff William McGahan escorted Peter Price from Butte to the Lewis and Clark County Jail.

Directed by County Attorney McConnell, the grand jury convened on Friday and ran a secret investigation for about one week. On Saturday, Peter Price was released on $1,000 bail. Community support for the vigilantes is revealed in the sureties for Price. The list reads like a "who's who" among community leaders: Thomas A. Marlow, president of the National Bank of Montana; real estate executive Reinhold H. Kleinschmidt; Jacob Fischer, president of the Helena Cab and Transfer Company; and wholesale/retail grocer Robert C. Wallace.

After interrogating thirty-eight witnesses, the grand jury finally released its finding on October 21. The jurors obviously faced the same stonewalling tactics from witnesses that had characterized the coroner's inquest—for they returned no indictments against specific vigilantes. The best they could produce was some strong censures:

> We must severely condemn the sheriff of Lewis and Clark County [Jeff O'Connell] for not having taken proper precaution to protect from mob violence the prisoner Brady, who was in his charge. . . . And we recommend the immediate dismissal of the night jailer George Mahrt, as he has shown himself incompetent and an unsafe man to hold so responsible a position.
>
> Further, we cannot too severely condemn the peace officers of the City of Helena and of the County of Lewis and Clark for having taken no steps after the lynching of Brady to ascertain who were the perpetrators of this crime.

Interestingly, Sheriff O'Connell ran for reelection in 1902 and won decisively. Despite the grand jury's recommendation, George Mahrt remained the county's night jailer until he retired in 1907. The county attorney dropped charges against Peter Price, and Hazel's father remained in Butte. Both Hazel and her mother recovered physically from their horrific experience at the hands of James Edward Brady, although the pair moved from Helena within a year.

So Helena's unidentified vigilantes escaped unpunished for their well-planned, precisely executed acts of unlawful defiance. Although an estimated 125 Helenans witnessed the break-in at the county jail and about 200 attended the subsequent hanging at Haymarket Square, not a single masked man was prosecuted.

The larger question of unlawful, vigilante justice—bowing to "Judge Lynch"—rightly engaged public officials, editorial writers, and ministers for months. Typical are the comments of the *Butte Inter Mountain:*

"That Brady, the wretch who was gibbeted in Helena, was not fit to live is a fact not to be denied. . . . However, in the cool light of reason, the affair cannot be defended. The law is supreme, and one violation of it does not justify another. . . . Mob violence is never defensible.

"If good citizens everywhere will elect competent and trustworthy men to office—and thus insure the proper performance of every public duty and public respect for the agencies of justice—there will be no mob violence in this state at any time."

The crime of James Edward Brady on little Hazel Price is a sordid tale. Just as reprehensible, however, are the actions of Helena's masked vigilantes during the early-morning hours of October 2, 1901. Little wonder that these shameful incidents have remained buried in the community's collective memory for so long.

~

Sources

The primary sources for this tale are Helena and area newspapers of the day. See particularly the *Helena Daily Independent,* the *Helena Daily Record,* the *Butte Inter Mountain,* and the *Butte Daily Miner.* Copies of Helena's third daily paper, the *Helena Evening Herald,* are not extant for October 1901. Transcripts from the pertinent coroner's jury and the grand jury could not be located in the Lewis and Clark County Courthouse.

The Life and Peculiar Death of "Long George" Francis

Dave Walter

*Oh, we all love our cowboys, so young
and so handsome.
We all love our cowboys, although
they do wrong.*

Montana-history jerks may be blatantly evil protagonists; misguided, bumbling oafs; or sneaky, slimy connivers. A jerk in Montana history may also be a person simply "caught out of time"—a historical misfit who plays by an outdated set of rules in a society that has moved on. "Long George" Francis epitomizes this category of anachronism, and he stretches its parameters wonderfully. On many levels, he functions as a solid Montana antihero.

Long George was just that: 6 feet 6 inches tall and about 190 pounds. To accent his slender height, George frequently wore a high-crowned ten-gallon Stetson. George had been known as "the Long Kid" until the early 1890s, when he rode into northern Montana. Since the area already had a "Short George," he became the logical antithesis. Later he became the perfect subject for a humorous sketch by Charlie Russell, who spotted the cowboy at the Havre Stampede in 1914.

George Francis was born in Utah on September 21, 1874. His father prospected, trapped, and ranched. When George was five, the family moved to southern Idaho, and he received some schooling. The combination of his unusual height and a deformed left hand caused George to learn the art of self-defense at an early age. As a youngster he read voraciously and learned to love horses—traits he maintained throughout his life.

In 1890, at the age of sixteen, George left home to escape the wrath of a domineering father, hiring on as a range hand for the large Warbonnet outfit in Idaho. When the ranch shipped a portion of its stock to the Bear's Paw area of northern Montana in 1893, George accompanied the herd.

Long George knew immediately that this Bear's Paw range was country in which he could make a life: vast stretches of open plains, sprawling herds of grazing cattle, and cow outfits that appreciated his expertise with a dancing rope and a savvy horse. George dreamed of establishing his own small ranch and running cattle and horses in the Havre area. The young man developed the characteristics of the archetypical open-range cowhand: friendliness, loyalty to his friends, pride in his work, proper respect for women and children, nonviolence except in the face of crisis, a willingness to help the needy, and an ability to handle difficult situations and survive. Atypically, George neither drank alcohol nor swore. He did smoke a pipe and the occasional cigarette.

Long George early held a weakness for flashy clothing, and he gained a reputation as "the best dressed cowboy in the Milk River country." He displayed "a penchant for fancy cowboy garb, shop-made, made-to-measure high-heeled boots, with his pant legs tucked into the fancy stitched tops, gay colored shirts, and the best beaver hat made by John B. Stetson."

George stayed with the Warbonnet until it folded in 1895 and then signed on for three years with the YT outfit, working in the Beaver Creek Valley. In 1897 the young cowhand broke his leg when a horse rolled on him. Thereafter he wore a longer heel on his right boot.

In 1898 George realized his goal of establishing his own ranch in the Bear's Paws. With this firm base, he proceeded to build a herd. His methods, though, raised suspicion among the locals. He was prone to branding mavericks, or "slicks," without regard for their origin. Others said that he might also be changing brands with a running iron. The code of the open range sometimes permitted the first activity, but it definitely frowned on the latter.

George, however, always had a quick explanation for his actions, and his congenial personality helped him duck the charges. In October 1904 a warrant was sworn out on Long George for horse theft. It later was dismissed for lack of evidence. Still, this was the same cowman who sent money home to his mother in Idaho when he had a bit extra.

Some ranchers in northern Montana suspected George of working with a gang that swapped stolen horses in Canada and the Dakotas. Strangely, he had little visible income, yet he possessed a growing herd of cattle and some really classy horses. Despite his open and friendly personality, Long George had developed enemies in the ranching community. They said that he "dragged a long rope with a maverick-hungry loop." Others charged that he was a "brand artist" who ran a "maverick factory."

In the fall of 1903 George left his ranch and became a constable in charge of the Havre animal pound and its garbage ordinance. He used this position as a stepping-stone to obtain a job as Havre's night marshal. Here he packed a show-gun: "a factory nickel-plated single action Colt .45, with a mother-of-pearl handle and a five-inch barrel."

Long George quickly became a distinctive figure on the streets of Havre; he was a cowboy and a range dude and a showman. His reputation as a debonair stockman grew when both the Havre and Great Falls newspapers published a love poem he had written to one of his paramours.

George was always clever with his hands and his mind. In 1903 he invented a metal gate opener for which he obtained an official U.S. patent. His creativity and affability—as well as the fact that he always carried candy to assuage his "sweet tooth"—drew children to him.

Long George resigned from the Havre police department in April 1907. He partnered up with Frank Reichel to run another horse and cattle ranch, this time 10 miles west of Havre. George's brand was the Pot Hook, or the Flying V. It rapidly began to appear on area mavericks—and on stock that his enemies said he had rustled.

Surprisingly, George continued to evade the law. One of his schemes entailed taking a rancher's horse and then "finding" him for the owner, returning the animal for a fee. Another gambit involved selling big, unbranded weaner calves to homesteaders and then rustling them back into his own herd before the buyers could get brands on them.

On the other hand, Long George's friends said that he was being credited with much mischief for which he was not responsible. He was called "a gentleman outlaw"—one who adhered to the open-range cowboy code but bent the law to help himself as well as the poor and the needy. Some went so far as to refer to Long George as "the Robin Hood of the Hi-Line." He surely did cultivate a following among some of the people of Hill County.

By 1912 it was clear that the influx of homesteaders to Montana's high plains spelled the end of the open-range days. As thousands of these honyockers fenced the range, built rural schools, imported automobiles, and voted for reform candidates to clean up vice, old-time cowhands like George lost their livelihoods and became cultural

Long George and Tony at The Great Northern Montana Stampede, Havre, 1913.
MONTANA HISTORICAL SOCIETY, HELENA.

anachronisms. George, however, astutely converted that displacement into nostalgia for the "Old West."

Long George had indulged in the relatively new sport of rodeo since early in the twentieth century. He developed as an outstanding steer-roper, bronc rider, and bulldogger—and he earned good prize money at it! He worked rodeos all along the Hi-Line and rode at the Pendleton (Oregon) Roundup and at the Calgary (Alberta) Stampede. George was the perfect fancy-dress cowboy who came to represent the Old West.

In steer-roping, Long George shared the spotlight with his favorite horse, Tony (named for movie idol Tom Mix's horse?). Tony, a big bay with a black mane and a white star on his forehead, became one of the finest cow-cutting horses on the rodeo circuit. George worked with Tony until the horse could do amazing tricks.

For example, when the steer was roped, thrown, and hog-tied in the arena, Tony kept the rope taut until George raised his hands for the benefit of the timer. Then the horse would slack the rope, approach the steer, and—placing one of his front hooves on the steer's ribs—shake his head up and down as George bowed himself to the crowd. The applause from the grandstands was deafening. Long George and the remarkable Tony built quite a reputation across Montana.

In 1913 George embarked on a career as a rodeo organizer. He soon managed cowboy contests in Alberta, Saskatchewan, and the Dakotas. By 1915 he was the president of the Great Northern Montana Stampede Association, and the 1916 Havre rodeo was the best ever. The charismatic cowboy was in his prime, at the age of forty-two.

By this time George had set his heart on an attractive school teacher who ran a one-room schoolhouse about 35 miles northwest of Havre, near the Canadian line. Amanda Spears became the focus of his attention and poetry, and they saw each other as frequently as they could.

In the fall of 1917, Long George was charged with grand larceny in the theft of a horse from Phil Clack. The controversy centered around a badly bungled rebranding of the mare with George's Flying V brand. George's many friends believed that this action was fabricated by George's enemies.

The trial began on February 25, 1918, and drew hundreds of spectators to the Hill County Courthouse. It was called "one of the most bitter trials in the annals of western range history." Authorities bent on reform argued mightily against George, attempting to make an object lesson of him. George's supporters countered with a well-reasoned defense. However, the jury of homesteaders deliberated for only ninety minutes before rendering a verdict of guilty. George was released on $5,000 bail to await sentencing on March 4.

But the cowman never appeared for the sentencing hearing! Instead he quietly packed up and rode out of town, jumping bail. On March 4 the judge declared Long George a fugitive, and the Hill County sheriff placed a $500 bounty on his head. The State of Montana contributed another $500 for a total bounty of $1,000. The widely distributed "wanted" poster carried a handsome photograph of the forty-five-year-old runaway.

For the next sixteen months, Long George was rumored to be holed up variously in the Bear's Paws, on a ranch near Big Sandy, in the Marias River country, in a dugout in the Little Rocky Mountains, or northwest of Havre along the Milk River. Despite the attractive reward, no one tried to bring him in, not even his enemies.

George said of this situation, "While I was gone from town a year and a half, and although there was a posted reward of $1,000 for my capture, no one that really wanted me dared come where I was. If twenty people were taken out of town, I could have returned and no one would have bothered me, because I was being persecuted, not prosecuted.

"As far as the matter of right is concerned, it's past and can never be recalled. But I still hate my enemies and love my friends. They were real friends that never quit fighting for me when they saw I was being railroaded for the personal spite of my enemies."

On July 8, 1919, George rode back into Havre on Tony and turned himself in to the county sheriff. The court imposed a sentence of six to twelve years for the original horse-theft grand larceny. Meanwhile George's attorneys petitioned for a new trial. The judge set George's new bail at $13,500, which thirteen of his friends quickly covered.

George's request for a new trial was denied by the Montana Supreme Court in December 1920. The district court remanded Long George to the state prison in Deer Lodge to serve his time. However, the stockman worked out a deal with the judge and the Hill County Sheriff. George would turn himself in on December 28 in Havre.

This timing allowed him to spend Christmas with his school-teacher fiancée, Amanda Spears. They planned to marry as soon as George returned from Deer Lodge. Then the couple would establish that little ranch that George so long had sought.

On Christmas Eve 1920, Long George borrowed a 1914 Hupmobile roadster from a friend and loaded his Christmas gifts for Amanda—particularly a large box of candy, a bag of nuts in their shells, and a crate of red apples. The apples were wrapped in a heavy blanket so that they would not freeze in the temperatures of thirty degrees below zero.

Despite what looked like an impending storm, George stopped at the barber shop before leaving Havre. He then followed a dim trail through the snow, trending northwest along the Milk River, headed for Amanda's schoolhouse. The icy blizzard hit when he was about 30 miles out of town, making his progress through the drifts agonizingly slow. Finally George lost the track completely, but he kept pushing on.

Suddenly, in the swirling snow, Long George backed out of a snowdrift, and his auto slipped over a steep, 12-foot cutbank. The auto tumbled downward onto the frozen Milk River channel. George was tossed from the vehicle, and it landed on top of his right leg, breaking it and pinning him to the ice. The shattered bone pierced the skin of his leg both front and back. George began to bleed onto the ice but managed to free himself from beneath the automobile.

Now George was faced with serious trouble. His leg continued to bleed; the blizzard intensified; he was at least 2 miles from the nearest shelter; and hypothermia was setting in. George ripped apart the apple crate and used its slats to splint his broken leg, tying the slats on with strips of blanket. Leaving his fancy pistol beneath the overturned vehicle, the courageous cowman began to drag himself along the ice toward the distant dugout.

Long George crawled almost a mile in the wind and the swirling snow before his strength gave out. His suffering must have been intense. Faced with a long and certain death, he used his pocket knife to slice twice into his neck to sever the jugular veins. He died quickly as the blizzard raged the rest of the day and through the night.

On the day after Christmas 1920, local farmer Ed Atkinson discovered the crumpled Hupmobile on the river ice. He investigated the wreck and then followed George's bloody trail up the river. In time he came upon the almost completely snow-covered body.

Atkinson piloted his horse-drawn sleigh into Havre to report the tragedy. The sheriff, the county coroner, and the local funeral director returned with the farmer to the death scene. They wrapped George's body in canvas and brought it back to Havre. At the subsequent inquest, the jury found that Long George had died "by loss of blood due to injuries received in an automobile accident and to wounds in the neck, self-inflicted."

Long George Francis's funeral convened at St. Mark's Episcopal Church in Havre on December 31, 1920. George's mother and brother attended, having arrived by train from Pocatello, Idaho. They joined Amanda Spears, there to mourn her beloved.

The funeral drew one of the greatest crowds in the history of Havre, and the procession to Highland Cemetery proved even larger. An unattended Tony dutifully followed the hearse, carrying an empty saddle, stirrups turned backward, with chaps and jingling spurs tied to the pommel. The Reverend Leonard Christler, who delivered the eulogy, perhaps said it best: "Game 'Long George' lived, and game 'Long George' died."

George Francis earns a jerk in Montana history title as an anachronism—an old-time open-range cowboy who was "caught out of time" in the homesteading era of the twentieth century. His personal code, his clothing, and his actions were embedded in a departed past, and he was unable to change. "Modern," reform-minded neighbors found those standards archaic, even criminal, and became George's enemies.

Long George's friends, on the other hand, revered his courage, his loyalty to friends, and his stockman's skills. This disparity in interpretation proved the crux of George's life and creates the essence of his jerk candidacy. For, as one biographer has noted, "The morning after Francis's body was brought in, many legends were born."

Perhaps author Walt Coburn stated the complexity of Long George Francis's story best: "The saga and legend of the colorful life of Long George Francis has been told and retold countless times at roundup camps and bunkhouses and winter line camps. It is still recounted, after nearly half a century of time, by old-timers wherever and whenever they meet. Yet nothing in the eventful, adventurous, brave life of George Francis became him like the leaving of it."

~

Sources

The definitive work on Long George Francis is a delightful volume written by Gary A. Wilson of Havre: *Tall in the Saddle: the "Long George" Francis Story, 1874–1920* (Helena: Falcon Press, 1989). The work embeds Francis in a detailed northern Montana context and provides wonderful descriptions of many of the friends and enemies of Long George. Wilson dodges none of the conflicts in which his subject became involved.

Two magazine pieces depict well the protagonist's character: Guy Weadick, "'Long George' Francis," *Canadian Cattlemen* (June 1945), 20–21, 25, 32–33; Walt Coburn, "Goodhearted and Unlucky," *Old West* (Spring 1968), 8–11, 60, 62.

These pieces can be supplemented with a bevy of newspaper articles of uneven quality. See, for example, *Montana Newspaper Association Inserts*, November 25, 1918; July 14, 1919; December 20, 1920; and January 10, 1921; "Long George, Hill County Anti-hero" (Havre) *Milk River Free Press*, July 9, 1975; "Pomp and Ceremony Featured Rites for Long George Francis" (Malta) *Phillips County News*, June 22, 1961; "Law and Order in the 'Good Old Days'" (Havre) *Hi-Line Herald*, March 29, April 5, and April 12, 1962; and "Met Untimely End on Christmas Eve," *Havre Daily News*, December 22, 1967.

Although court records are extant for several of the entanglements of Long George, local newspapers provide perhaps the most detailed specifics on the range of public events in his life. See the *Havre Plaindealer*, 1902–1921; the *Havre Herald*, 1904–1908; the *Havre Weekly Promoter*, 1909–1915; the *Havre Daily Promoter*, 1916–1918, 1920–1921; and the (Havre) *Hill County Democrat*, 1912–1921.

Patriots Gone Berserk:
The Montana Council of Defense, 1917–1918
Dave Walter

*Fix it so that no longer may the enemy spies or the ped-
dlers of sedition and slander go free in Montana—to
insult the patriotism and to offend the loyalty of our
citizens at home or send cheer to the enemy abroad. . . .
We are today either loyal citizens of this, our native or
adopted land, or else we are traitors. The neutral or
"half baked" citizen, in time of war, is an impossible
conception.*

Governor Samuel V. Stewart, 1918

DURING WORLD WAR I, THE MONTANA COUNCIL OF DEFENSE WROTE ONE
of the very darkest chapters in Montana history.

Under the mantle of "wartime emergency" and "protecting the
public safety," the Council played fast and loose with the civil liberties
of all Montanans, imposing restrictions that today seem preposter-
ous—clear violations of constitutionally guaranteed rights. And the
Council did it all by trading on the war's rampant emotionalism and
by cloaking itself in "patriotism" and "100% Americanism."

For almost two years, the Montana Council of Defense served as
a parallel state government: one that set its own rules, answered to no
higher authority, and seized and practiced all three functions of government—legislative, judicial, and executive. Further, the Council's
"reign of terror" took a serious toll on Montana society for years after
the war.

World War I began in Europe in 1914. However, the United States
did not enter the conflict until April 6, 1917. During the intervening
years, Montanans hotly debated war issues that included:

• Should the United States enter this foreign war?

• Should the United States bankroll the Allies in the interim?

- Does the Constitution allow the United States to send draftees overseas?

On the American home front, a growing wave of hyperpatriotism grew into anti-German fanaticism and even "German bashing." And with the entry of the United States into the war, that fervor swept across Montana—Montanans jumped into the war effort with both feet. About 40,000 of the state's young men either enlisted or were drafted into service. With booming grain markets and top prices, Montana farmers borrowed to the hilt to expand their acreage. Statewide Liberty bond drives and Red Cross subscriptions regularly exceeded their quotas. Butte miners (when not on strike) worked three continuous shifts, seven days a week. All of Montana's newspapers were flooded with war news, both from abroad and from the home front.

In this context President Woodrow Wilson asked state governors and state legislatures to create "state councils of defense"—somewhat along the lines of the National Council of Defense. He directed the state councils to:

- Increase food production.
- Recruit men for the draft.
- Raise money for war drives.
- Promote public support for the war.

But in Montana the 1917 Legislature recently had adjourned. So Governor Sam V. Stewart created the Montana Council of Defense by executive proclamation. Thus the Council held no legislated authority; it was really just a "governor's advisory panel."

The state's initial Council of Defense well represented Montana's upper middle class. It contained two bankers, a university president, two mercantile executives, a newspaper editor, and a token woman. Governor Stewart appointed *himself* as chairman of the Council, and he designated his head of the Department of Agriculture and Publicity—Charles D. Greenfield—as the Council's executive secretary.

Since there was neither legislative authorization nor an appropriation, none of the Council members was paid. The Council's expenses would be covered out of other state-government funds. The State Council quickly created supporting councils in every one of Montana's forty-three counties. Each county council comprised three men appointed by the governor and the State Council and held the same powers as did the State Council.

In addition, the county councils could certify subordinate town and district groups—"community councils." These local committees were *open to anyone who wished to join*—and thus drew the most extreme "patriots." The committees did not, however, hold the powers of their superior councils.

It would be these community councils that became the "third-degree committees": the self-styled watchdogs of a community's standards of "Americanism" and the harassers of those neighbors whom they found "un-American."

During the early months of the Montana Council of Defense's existence, wartime hysteria raged in the state. In the throes of extreme emotionalism, citizens learned quickly how to use the Council to their advantage. You could settle any old grudge simply by reporting your personal enemy to the county council—and then sit back and watch your fanatical neighbors go after one of their own!

For example, a teacher in Rexford (Lincoln County) had offended the parents of several of his students. The adults reported him to the Lincoln County Council of Defense, and J. M. Kennedy of the county council wrote to State Council Secretary Greenfield about the teacher:

"He is not a good citizen. He is disloyal to this country. He is a rabid, arrogant rebel. He persistently refuses to do his duty as a citizen. As a teacher of the public school at Rexford, he is a public menace. Always he preaches and teaches dangerous doctrines."

Dragged before the county council in Libby, the teacher would admit only to refusing to aid in a campaign to sell thrift and war stamps in the Rexford school. He maintained that children should not be taught that war was worthy of their financial support.

Within two weeks, minutes of the Libby inquiry were delivered to the State Council in Helena. The instructor's teaching certificate then was revoked by the State Superintendent of Public Instruction, and he was fired by the local school board.

To combat Montana's growing wartime problems (both real and imagined), Governor Stewart finally called a special session of the Montana Legislature for February 14, 1918. In a frenzy of fanatical patriotism, legislators passed a statewide gun-registration law and an exceptionally tough espionage law.

They also approved an incredible sedition law, with penalties running to a fine of $20,000 and/or twenty years in jail. Because of its

STOP malicious rumors —Help win the war!

Courtesy of Century Co.   Louis Raemaekers

What kind of an American is this?

An Appeal to Loyal Americans
from the
National Committee of Patriotic Societies
ILLUSTRATIONS BY LOUIS RAEMAEKERS

"Sowing the Seeds of Sedition" sketch, pamphlet published by
National Committee of Patriotic Societies.

severity, this legislation became the core of the *federal* sedition law later in the year—another dubious honor for Montana.

Special-session legislators also passed a bill that officially created the Council of Defense and made it a legitimate state agency. The legislation appropriated $25,000 for operating expenses and directed the Council to dispense $500,000 in federal seed loans to farmers. In light of gaining official sanction, the Council reorganized its membership.

The new (second) Council really had gained incredible power— its enabling legislation permitted it to do "*anything* not contradicted by the U.S. Constitution or the Montana Constitution." An extralegal body that already had operated for ten months became a legal entity with vast authority.

The legislature granted the State Council the power to create "bylaws" or "orders" to regulate Montana's wartime situation. Breaking one of these orders drew a fine of $1,000, or one year in jail, or both! Violators of these "laws" were prosecuted by county attorneys and processed through the state courts.

Rapidly the new Council set to work creating orders: seventeen in seven months! Most of these laws limited or prohibited an activity or a right that the Council deemed "antipatriotic" or "detrimental to the war effort." They ran the gamut, from banning parades, to prohibiting fires, to forbidding use of the German language in Montana schools and churches.

Two of the most important orders were numbers 7 and 8, by which the Council *gave itself* the powers to investigate, to subpoena, and to punish violators. It could hold hearings and compel witnesses to attend. It could fine violators and even imprison them. And it did just that in the cases of suspected German operatives Eberhardt von Waldru and Oscar Rohn. Likewise the Council publicly and repeatedly investigated William Dunne, the editor of the radical *Butte Bulletin.*

Just as frightening, the powers invested in the State Council extended to the county councils. So rabid county-level "patriots" also could drag their neighbors before an intimidating county panel and grill them *on any subject they wanted.*

The second Montana Council of Defense continued its original tasks of increasing farm production, filling draft quotas, and promoting fund drives. But more and more it moved into the realm of "creating and maintaining emotional support for the war effort." That is, it whipped Montanans into a pro-American, anti-German frenzy.

Simultaneously it spread fear throughout Montana society by wielding its self-appointed investigative and punitive powers.

The State Council's favorite targets were Socialists (especially members of the radical Industrial Workers of the World and the liberal Nonpartisan League), pacifists, Montana's German-Russian population, Mennonites (who, unfortunately, were both pacifist and German), and suspected German sympathizers of *any* ethnic background.

The Council kept secret dossiers on "suspicious citizens" and tried, unsuccessfully, to create a 400-man state police force, attached to the Council. Either with the enthusiastic support of Montanans or with their acquiescence (often based in fear), the Council controlled everyday life in Montana. And its victims had no recourse—for the Council answered to no one. Mass hysteria and ethnic intolerance fueled Montana's hyperpatriotism.

Some of the greatest violations of civil liberties occurred during "investigations" run by the county councils. Executive Secretary Greenfield described such an instance involving men who had "undersubscribed" to a Red Cross fund drive in Broadwater County: "In two cases, these men were brought before the Broadwater County Council of Defense and, while they first persisted in their original decision [not to contribute], nevertheless public sentiment was so stirred up against them that they finally concluded that it was the best part of wisdom to subscribe to the fund drive.

"In one case, a genteel boycott was put on a man, in that he was not spoken to by any of his old friends. When he went into a store, the proprietor refused to allow him to be waited on. It took only about 24 hours of this sort of treatment to bring this gentleman to his senses."

Community councils also ran rampant. These groups of self-appointed "patriots" created "standards of Americanism" and used them to monitor local actions. Neighbors suspected of pro-German sympathies frequently were brought to the steps of the county courthouse or the city hall. Here—to publicly demonstrate their patriotism—they were forced to kiss the flag, to sing all the verses of "God Bless America," or to recite the Pledge of Allegiance ten times.

Both county and community councils also practiced "the delimiting of civil liberties in the name of patriotism" with visiting speakers from suspect organizations. In Miles City Nonpartisan League organizer J. A. "Mickey" McGlynn was surrounded by members of the local Third Degree Committee as he stepped off the train one afternoon.

Courtesy of Century Co.   **Louis Raemaekers**

The rats in our home trenches

"Rats" sketch, pamphlet published by National Committee of Patriotic Societies.

The "patriots" hustled McGlynn to the basement of a nearby hotel, where they beat him severely. Committee members then dumped him on the next express to Billings, with the admonition that "Nonpartisan League talk has *no* place in Miles City." When State Attorney General Sam C. Ford attempted to bring these thugs to task, he was thwarted by the Custer County Attorney, who refused to pursue the case.

Once the anti-German hysteria took root in Montana, it proved hard to control. In the name of "Americanism," community and county councils pursued any citizens they considered nonconformists "to make them part of the community's war effort." In Burton K. Wheeler's autobiography, *Yankee from the West*, the U.S. Senator remarks:

> In the fall of 1917, so-called "Liberty Committees" were organized in most of the small towns of the state to deal directly with anyone accused of being pro-German or who refused to buy the number of Liberty Bonds that these committees would assess against an individual as his "quota."
>
> The owner of a Billings meat market, who had torn up his Liberty Loan subscription blank, was forced to kiss the flag.
>
> According to the *Anaconda Standard,* a so-called "Third Degree Committee" in Billings rounded up "pro-Germans and financial slackers" there in November 1917. A Billings City Council member also was forced to resign his job and to carry an American flag through the streets [to prove his patriotism].

Some of the most vexing violations of rights guaranteed to Americans by their Constitution resulted from Order #3, forbidding the use of the German language. In fact, even before the enactment of Order #3, anti-German fanatics had run Montana's last German-language paper, the (Helena) *Montana Staats-Zeitung,* out of business. The weekly folded in September 1916, after these "patriots" had harassed its advertisers into submission.

Order #3 immediately halted the teaching of the German language in Montana schools, both public and private. The order listed a series of "pro-German" books to be removed from the shelves of all school libraries and public libraries. In Lewistown, Brockway, and at the University of Montana in Missoula, "suspect" books were burned

NON-WORKER'S REGISTRATION CARD

This is to Certify that_____,

who registered on the_____ day of_____191 ,
under order No. Two, of the Montana Council of Defense, as a non-
worker, gives as a reason for his non employment the following:

_____

_____

_____

County Clerk and Recorder.

Dated at_____ 1

Non-worker's registration card.
ORIGINAL FROM AUTHOR'S PERSONAL COLLECTION.

in public bonfires. The librarian at Hilger, a community northeast of Lewistown, wrote to the State Council:

"Last month we weeded out all german [sic] texts that were in our school library, clipped out all german songs in our books of national songs, blotted out the coat of arms and the german flags in the dictionaries, and urged that every home should destroy the german-text and [banned] library books that they possess. We also spell 'germany' without a capital letter.

"A few days ago, we burned all of our *West's Ancient Worlds* [one of the texts on the Council's banned list], and I have the permission of our school trustees to destroy *any* texts found to contain german propaganda."

Order #3 also banned the use of German from the pulpit. This decision—from which the State Council never wavered—devastated a number of German-language congregations in eastern Montana, particularly Lutherans, Congregationalists, Mennonites, and Hutterites.

In heart-wrenching letters to the State Council, ministers pleaded for *some* modification of Order #3. For example, Lutheran pastor H. E. Vomhof of Laurel in 1918 wrote to the Council's secretary Greenfield:

"I am coming to you in the interest of my congregation. It consists of Russians of the Volga district. Many of them, especially the old people, are not able to speak a word of English, and they understand very little. Of a sermon preached in English, the majority understand nothing but the words 'God,' 'Jesus,' and 'amen,' or the names of the Apostles when mentioned. . . .

"Now, my desire is that you ask the Council to allow us to have our communion services—also the funeral services—in German. To partake of the Lord's Supper without understanding what is said would be sinful. Hence we cannot celebrate the Lord's Supper—although that celebration is allowed and guaranteed us by the Constitution of the United States. . . .

"Remember, I do not desire to have *all* services in German. I do not ask for more than the above mentioned, although I believe that the worshiping of the people in any language should be left free—war or no war."

When some congregations began to meet in private homes rather than in churches to worship in German, the State Council specifically banned *that* practice. Even after the war was over (November 11, 1918), the Council punitively held fast to its ban forbidding German in Montana churches.

Perhaps most frightening about the actions of the high-handed state, county, and community councils is that they practiced their peculiar brand of "100% Americanism" on their own neighbors! Friend turned on friend; family turned on family; communities were shredded by suspicion, threats, and bizarre actions—all in the name of "patriotism."

Because it was so strongly emotional, there simply was no way to stop this white-hot hysteria on Armistice Day. The ethnic hatred and divisiveness continued well into the early 1920s. For most Montanans, the hysteria finally played out then, but some of the hard-core purveyors of intolerance moved into the Montana Realm of the Ku Klux Klan, officially founded in 1923.

Interestingly, the 1918 enabling legislation for the Montana Council of Defense required it to dissolve three months after the signing of a treaty. But problems developed among State Council members in interpreting what constituted a "treaty signing," so the Council existed, at least on paper, until Governor Joseph M. Dixon finally killed it on August 24, 1921.

But by then the damage to Montana society had been done. World War I's patriotic madness had poisoned an entire generation of

Montanans. It certainly affected the state's German-descent victims. But it also changed the anti-German fanatics, who either attacked their neighbors or said nothing when those attacks were made.

All of this home front violence and "delimitation of Constitutional liberties" falls at the feet of the Montana Council of Defense. This agency acted as a parallel state government in Montana for almost two years—some of this time in a *completely* extralegal capacity.

The State Council organized and fed the hatred and the hysteria. It set the pattern for county councils and community councils. And it generally condoned—even justified—the extreme actions of those subordinates. In an attempt to support the war effort to bring liberty and democracy to Europe, the Montana Council of Defense destroyed the liberty and democracy of Montanans at home.

Does the story of the Montana Council of Defense have anything to teach us today? The response obviously is "yes." That is one of the reasons we study history!

Given the right circumstances, similar violations of our civil rights could occur again. We need to be watchful, and we need to be vocal. The actions of the Montana Council of Defense constitute one of the very darkest chapters in the Montana story. That it happened here once is more than enough.

~

Sources

The core source for this chapter is the extensive collection of papers: Record Series 19: Montana Council of Defense, 1916–1921, Montana Historical Society Archives, Helena. This material can be supplemented with the pertinent state *Laws and Resolutions* passed by the 1917 legislature in regular and extraordinary sessions and by the state document *Proceedings of the Court for the Trial of Impeachment: the People of the State of Montana . . . v. Charles L. Crum . . .* (Helena: State Publishing, 1919).

Periodical pieces that apply include O. A. Hilton, "Public Opinion and Civil Liberties in Wartime, 1917–1919," *Southwestern Social Science Quarterly*, 28 (1955), 32–48; Benjamin Rader, "The Montana Lumber Strike of 1917," *Pacific Historical Review*, 36 (May 1967), 189–207; Hugh T. Lovin, "World War Vigilantes in Idaho, 1917–1918," *Idaho Yesterdays*, 18, #3 (Fall 1974), 2–11; and Anna Zellick, "Patriots on the Rampage: Mob Action in Lewistown, 1917–1918," *Montana: the Magazine of Western History*, 31, #1 (Winter 1981), 30–43. See especially Arnon Gutfeld, *Montana's Agony: Years of War and Hysteria, 1917–1921* (Gainesville: University Presses of Florida, 1973).

Much work in this field remains buried in honors papers and theses. See particularly Charles S. Johnson, "Two Montana Newspapers—the *Butte Bulletin* and the *Helena Independent*—and the Montana Council of Defense, 1917–1921," B.A. Honors Paper, University of Montana, 1970; Charles S. Johnson, "An Editor and a War: Will A. Campbell and the *Helena Independent,* 1914–1921," M.A. thesis, University of Montana, 1977; Kurt Wetzel, "The Making of an American Radical: Bill Dunne in Butte," M.A. thesis, University of Montana, 1970; Timothy C. McDonald, "The Montana Press and American Neutrality in the First World War," M.A. seminar paper, University of Montana, 1975; Mark Mackin, "The Council for Defense: Autocracy in Montana, 1917–1918," B.A. Honors Paper, Carroll College, 1976; and Arnon Gutfeld, "The Butte Labor Strikes and Company Retaliation during World War I," M.A. thesis, University of Montana, 1967. See especially Nancy Rice Fritz, "The Montana Council of Defense," M.A. thesis, University of Montana, 1966.

The other rich source of color for this chapter is Montana's statewide array of newspapers—particularly the *Butte Daily Bulletin* and the *Helena Independent.*

In League with the Devil:
Boone Helm and "Liver-Eatin' Johnston"
Jon Axline

CONSIDERED BY MANY TO BE THE "LAST TABOO," CANNIBALISM HAS BECOME a popular topic for western authors. Many books have been published describing horrific true tales of survival where the unfortunate protagonists were reduced to the cannibalization of their comrades and traveling companions to stay alive. Cannibalism is in fact an oft-repeated theme in the American West. Few Americans have not heard the tragic tale of the Donner Party's sojourn in the Sierra Madre Mountains during the brutal winter of 1846–1847 or of Alferd Packer's efforts to put a significant dent in the number of Democrats in Hinsdale County, Colorado, by dining on five men during an aborted prospecting trip in the Rocky Mountains in 1874. These stories are meant to remind us that even the most "normal" of us will take extraordinary steps to survive. Although the history of the Old West is full of sterling examples of humanity, there are also a few monsters lurking in the shadows, some of them with rather heinous gastronomical habits.

Montana has had its share of cannibals, ranging from frontier days to the 1970s, when Montanans were shocked to learn the grisly details of crimes committed near Livingston and in the Gallatin Valley. Some of these men became cannibals to survive, while others were criminals who killed and ate their victims for pleasure. Mid-nineteenth-century Montana hosted two men who based their reputations on the eating of human flesh: Boone Helm and John Johnston, aka "Liver-Eatin' Johnston." While one boasted of his culinary deviation, the other was infamous by reputation rather than actual deed.

Next to Henry Plummer and George Ives, Boone Helm was the most notorious member of the alleged road agent gang that terrorized Bannack and Virginia City in the early 1860s. Indeed, Helm is the only one who even vigilante revisionists believe may actually have deserved his fate on the scaffold. Even without his foray into the world of man-eating, Helm would have deserved the title of jerk. He was a loudmouthed braggart, a wife-beater, and an unrepentant murderer. Born to Joseph and the unnamed Mrs. Helm in Kentucky in 1826 or 1827, Boone had twelve brothers and sisters. Although the family was by no means wealthy, it enjoyed a rock-solid reputation for honesty and hard work in Monroe County, Missouri, where the family relocated in 1831.

By all accounts, Helm enjoyed an almost idyllic childhood on the Missouri frontier. Described by some as a "little wild," with coarse features and a heavy build, Helm built a name for himself as an excellent horseman and marksman. When not jumping his horse off a bridge into the Salt River, he could hurl a knife while on horseback and then retrieve the still quivering weapon from the ground at full gallop. In 1851 he married seventeen-year-old Lucinda Browning. Within a short time, however, Helm's exuberance and fondness for hard liquor and carousing with the boys wore thin with her. He would, according to Lucinda, frequently ride his horse into their house and keep it there for hours. It was also rumored that Helm frequently beat his young wife after binging in the local saloons.

In the fall of 1852, after a bitter fight with Lucinda, Helm accused a boyhood friend of stealing a $10 gold piece from him. Although accounts differ, witnesses agree that Helm visited his friend's cabin later that night, called him outside, and fatally stabbed the man. Helm fled the area for Indian Territory, where he was arrested shortly thereafter. When he was returned to Missouri, his wife divorced him on grounds of cruelty. On a positive note for Helm, none of the witnesses called against him appeared in court, and the murder charges were dropped. In the process, however, he bankrupted his father (who had paid the costs of the divorce) and ruined the family's reputation in Monroe County. Helm left Missouri and headed west in 1852 or 1853.

Accounts of Helm's life over the next several years differ, but they are colorful to say the least. After leaving Missouri he joined a band of California horse thieves; performed covert executions for Brigham Young (perhaps even participating in the Mountain Meadows Massacre in 1857); stole military livestock in Lodi, California; robbed a storekeeper in Los Angeles; broke jail in Oregon; and survived a shipwreck only to attempt to steal his rescuer's livestock. Helm had clearly chosen the wrong path on the road of human endeavor.

It was during the winter of 1859 that Helm became a cannibal under circumstances that echoed other cases of the Last Taboo. He and his companions were caught unprepared in a snowstorm. In October 1859 Helm, a boyhood friend named Elijah Barton, and five others bought a racehorse at The Dalles, Oregon, with the intent of taking it to Salt Lake City to race. When the company reached southwestern Idaho, they were attacked by Cayuse Indians. Fleeing, they made camp three days later but were attacked again, this time losing one of their number. Bad luck continued to plague the party when they were beset by an early-season blizzard. After stumbling around for a few days, the men found shelter in an abandoned cabin. The blizzard continued to rage, however, and they were forced to slaughter all their horses for food, including the prized racehorse. The party set out again for Fort Hall, with Helm and Barton eventually leaving their companions behind. By the time the pair reached the fort, which they found abandoned, Barton was snow-blind and too weak to go on. Here the story becomes somewhat confused. While Helm later told his fellow saloon patrons that Barton committed suicide when it became clear to him they couldn't go on, rumors also circulated that he murdered the man to provide himself with provisions.

Regardless of how Elijah Barton died, Helm saw opportunity in the corpse, reportedly cutting slices of meat from the dead man's legs and wrapping them in a dirty flannel shirt. Helm then continued on his way to Salt Lake City. He spent a few weeks with an Indian family, who charged him room and board to share their tepee. Helm repaid their generosity by sharing his "provisions" with them. By the time Helm reached a freighting outpost in Utah in April 1859, his rations had nearly run out. He reportedly threw what remained of his boyhood pal to a dog, boasting of what kind of meat had supported him for the past few months.

After being "expelled from the Salt Lake valley for his atrocities," Helm drifted west and north, leaving a trail of "villainies," including murder and robbery, behind him. He reached Florence, Idaho, by October 1862. While partying in a saloon there, he challenged a miner by the name of "Dutch Fred" to a fight. Patrons of the saloon broke it up, and Helm left the establishment. He returned a short time later, borrowed a revolver, and fatally shot Fred.

Helm fled the camp and headed north into British Columbia, where he was seen trapping on the Frazer River with a man named Angus MacPherson. Several months later, he was arrested in the Adelphia Saloon in a Frazer River mining camp for refusing to pay for his drinks. When asked by the owner to pay, Helm replied, "Don't you know that I'm a desperate character?" Unfazed, the proprietor of the establishment called the local constable, who arrested Helm. When questioned about MacPherson, Helm allegedly replied, "Why, do you suppose that I'm a damn fool enough to starve to death when I can help it? I ate him up of course!"

After serving a month in the local jail, Helm drifted back to the United States, where he was arrested at Florence for the murder of Dutch Fred. Again, no one could be found to testify against him, and the murder charges were dropped. Helm worked for a time as a miner with his brother before drifting to the mining camps in Montana Territory.

The story of Boone Helm then becomes part of Montana folklore. Arrested in Virginia City on January 14, 1864, he was hanged along with four other alleged road agents and buried on boot hill. Unlike his comrades, however, Helm was consigned to his fate and exited the stage with same aplomb that characterized his colorful and brutal life—with an admonition and a cheer for the losing side: "Every man for his principles! Hurrah for Jeff Davis! Let 'er rip!" Indeed, Boone Helm had a warped sense of principles: murder, mayhem, debauchery, and cannibalism.

If there was ever an individual who looked like a cannibal, it was John Johnston. Known affectionately, but incorrectly, as "Liver Eatin' Johnston" after 1870, he, like Calamity Jane and John X. Beidler, is known more by reputation than by actual deed. Not a particularly outgoing individual, he let his admirers embellish stories about his exploits, seldom, if ever, denying them—even if they were patently untrue. Unlike Boone Helm, an avowed cannibal, Johnston was a cannibal by reputation only.

Born on the East Coast in the early 1820s, Johnston shipped out on a whaling vessel sometime in the late 1830s. In 1843 he reputedly enlisted in the U.S. Navy but jumped ship after coldcocking an officer. From then until the outbreak of the Civil War, his history is virtually unknown. He did drift west after his short stint in the Navy. He may have attached himself to an old mountain man named Hatcher to learn the fur trade, several years after its golden age had ended. He joined the Union Army in Colorado in 1864, participating in several battles on the western frontier before his discharge in 1865. This is where his legend begins.

Reportedly during one of the battles of Newtonia in Missouri,

Liver-Eatin' Johnston, ca.1876–1877.
PHOTOGRAPH BY JOHN H. FOUCH, BLACK HILLS, DAKOTA TERRITORY.
MONTANA HISTORICAL SOCIETY, HELENA.

Johnston began killing Indians but did not differentiate whose side they were on. After a reprimand by General J. A. Blunt, he was returned to duty. Soon after, he was caught scalping dead Confederate soldiers. Despite these eccentricities, he was honorably discharged by the Army and returned to Montana Territory. By 1869 he was working as a wood hawk at the pretentiously named Kerchival City, a collection of rude log cabins surrounded by a stockade near the mouth of the Musselshell River.

In March 1869 Johnston and fourteen others were ambushed by Blackfeet or Lakota warriors while cutting wood outside the fort's stockade. In the ensuing battle, several Indians were killed by the besieged wood hawks. It was in the aftermath of this fight that Johnston gained his reputation as a man-eater, although accounts differ as to the actual event. One story states that a tenderfoot participant in the battle entered a cabin where Johnston was cooking deer liver over an open fire. The man asked Johnston where he got it. He replied, "No use going hungry with so many dead Indians around."

Another story, which seems to be corroborated by Johnston himself, is much more gruesome. After killing a young warrior, he cut out a piece of the luckless man's liver. Johnston was supposed to have said:

> Just then a sort of squeamish old fellow named Ross came running up. I waved the knife with the liver on it in the air and I cried out "Come on and have a piece! It'll stay yer stomach 'til you get home to dinner!"
>
> "Don't want non," sez he.
>
> "Come on," sez I, dancing around, "I've ett some and its just as good as antelope's liver. Have a bite." Then Ross he threw up his guts. And he always swore after that he seen me tear a liver out of a dyin' Injun and eat it. But that ain't so. I was all over blood and I had the liver on my knife, but I didn't eat none of it.

With variations, this is the story that was most commonly repeated about Johnston. Yet another popular version states that after cutting the liver out of a dead Indian, Johnston, his face covered in blood, held up a piece of the liver stuck on his knife and said, "Do any of you fellas take your liver raw?"

Several months after the disputed liver incident, the steamboat *Huntsville* landed at Kerchival City and the passengers were greeted by a nightmarish scene. Readers were later treated to a newspaper account of it that included a hellish description of Johnston himself:

> At the end of the line of skulls stood the old trapper himself, Liver-eating Johnson, and a queer sight he was on that day. He was leaning on a crutch. The day was especially warm so the amount of his clothing was in accordance. The much shrunken and faded old red undershirt was scant and barely reached below his hips, and was absolutely all he wore. One leg was bandaged. His hair was long and uncombed. His beard was bushy and fluttered in the hot breeze. He was a huge man, and with so very much of his big frame exposed to view he made a characteristic picture that those passengers never could forget.

Stories about Johnston were legion. Like John X. Beidler and Calamity Jane, he seemed to be everywhere at once. With each telling, the legend overshadowed the reality of the man. Even today, it is difficult to distinguish who the real Liver-Eatin' Johnston was—to separate fact from fiction. Even revered Montana writer and historian Dorothy Johnson got caught up in the myth. In her 1973 book with Reverend R. T. Turner, *The Bedside Book of Bastards,* she repeats many of the Johnston myths, including an unsubstantiated story about cannibalism involving the leg of a Blackfoot warrior that sounds very much like it was borrowed from Boone Helm's life. It could be, however, that she just recognized a good story. Johnston was a good man to avoid—a bastard in the best sense of the word.

As the Wild West became tamer in the late nineteenth century, Johnston increasingly relied on his reputation to survive and, in the process, became a true frontier "character." For a time he worked in a Wild West show as the "Avenging Fury of the Plains," before the show went broke in Iowa. His reputation and alleged appetite for liver served him well in Coulson and Red Lodge, where he worked in law enforcement. In Coulson he kept the peace mostly with his fists; in Red Lodge he kept it through his reputation. Sometimes a reputation for cannibalism, even if it never happened, can work to your benefit.

John Johnston died in an old soldiers home in California in 1900. He remained largely forgotten until the post–World War II renaissance in Western history. In 1958 Raymond W. Thorp and Robert Bunker published *Crow Killer,* an attempt to make Johnston germane to the late twentieth century. The book, however, repeats many of the false-hoods about Johnston's life—especially the cannibalism. In 1969 Vardis Fisher published *Mountain Man,* a popular novelized "biography" of John Johnston. Robert Redford played the old reprobate in the movie version of the book, *Jeremiah Johnson,* in 1972. Although the motion picture was loosely based on John Johnston's life, there was some element of truth to it—the historical figure did live in the West. Curiously, an article published in *Montana Magazine* in 1981 passes off the Kerchival City incident as true and trivializes the reason Fisher changed Johnston's name from John to Jeremiah. Liver-Eatin' Johnston has become a character that molds together both fact and fiction.

In 1926 former plainsman Sylvester Whalen called Johnston a "bad Indian fighter," killing more Indians around the campfire than he did in battle. He added that men like Johnston were most dangerous when standing behind an unarmed foe. He concluded:

> It is the liver-eating variety of citizen who caused the friction between the Indians and the whites, which turmoil resulted in the sacrifice of innumerable lives and the needless torture of hundreds of human beings.

Even his admiring biographer, Raymond Thorp, was forced to admit that Johnston was "capable of little love and even less compassion for his Indian enemies." Indeed, in 1889 Johnston left poisoned meat outside his tent. Lakota warriors ate some of it and died an agonizing death, much to Johnston's delight. Although he was not a cannibal, Johnston was truly a wretched individual.

In many ways, Boone Helm and Liver-Eatin' Johnston are representative of what many people like to believe were true frontier characters. Even forgetting his taste in meat, Helm was the quintessential Western bad man. Despite his admonition to lead a principled life when he was executed for his crimes in 1864, he had no apparent redeeming qualities. He was unrepentant and loved life as an outlaw and social outcast. He does not even seem a suitable candidate for Henry Plummer's well-organized gang of road agents. He was boorish, a braggart, and morally bankrupt. No one could argue that he wasn't a jerk.

Liver-Eatin' Johnston presents a different problem. Like Calamity Jane and John X. Beidler, he has evolved into a true Montana celebrity—and a hero to some. While he may not have eaten anybody's liver, he still did some depraved things during his life and epitomized the very essence of the slob Indian fighter. Some might say that he did what he did to survive and that it's not our place to judge him according to twenty-first century standards. However, it can also be argued that debauched behavior transcends time—what was reprehensible conduct on the Montana frontier 130 years ago is still just as reprehensible today.

Helm and Johnston were colorful frontier characters. A cannibal and a murderer, however, do not make for good role models. Nor do they represent the majority of people who came to Montana in the late nineteenth century. They took survival to the extreme and lived by their own rules. No doubt, they are the stuff of Western legend, but the cost was high in men mutilated, murdered, and cannibalized. These two based their careers on crimes gleefully committed against their fellow man.

~

Sources

Although he is one of Montana's best-known outlaws, there is surprisingly little written about Boone Helm. R. E. Mather and F. E. Boswell's *Vigilante Victims: Montana's 1864 Hanging Spree* (History West, 1991) provides good and hitherto unknown information about Helm's early life in Missouri and his exile from the state after murdering his neighbor. Contemporary newspaper sources in Idaho and British Columbia fill in the gap between his exit from Missouri and his arrival in the Montana mining camps. Thomas Dimsdale's *Vigilantes of Montana* is the standard history of Henry Plummer's road agent gang and its members' fate at the hangman's noose. Nathaniel Pitt Langford's *Vigilante Days and Ways* reiterates much of Dimsdale's apologia but also adds additional information about the road agents' backgrounds, including Boone Helm. The vertical files at the Montana Historical Society also contain considerable information about Helm. Some appear to be accurate, and some don't fit with the established facts of Helm's life and career. It all, however, makes for interesting reading.

Information about Liver-Eatin' Johnston is legion, although mostly inaccurate. He was mostly venerated as a frontier hero in the Montana press in the twentieth century. But buried among the fluff about him in the vertical files at the Montana Historical Society are more than a few less-than-complimentary observations about Johnston by his contemporaries. Most of what remains about his life was written after his death in 1900. The Liver Eater usually appears as a supporting character in a number of books about the Old West. Mostly it's flattering, and little of it jibes with other references. Raymond W. Thorp's *Crow Killer: The Saga of Liver-Eating Johnson* (Amereon, 1980) is not accurate in many respects, in that it repeats the legends more than the facts. Vardis Fisher's *Mountain Man* (William Morrow, 1965) is a fictional account of Johnston's life on which the movie *Jeremiah Johnson* was based. To obtain an accurate portrayal of Liver-Eatin' Johnston's life, its best to read the available sources carefully—and between the lines.

Poison Pen: Will Campbell, Helena's Notorious Newspaper Editor

Jon Axline

In the days before radio and television, newspapers were, for most Americans, the only source of international, national, and local news. Newspaper editors enjoyed a special status in communities, based on their control of the media. The editor determined what would be included in that day's edition and how it would be presented to its readers. Like the media today, those early spin doctors were far from unbiased about the information they provided and much less subtle about how it was presented. There was never any question about what they thought about political, social, or community issues. They saw them in black-and-white terms—there was no gray area and often no room for dissension. You either agreed with them and bought their newspapers or you were against them and suffered their displeasure in a most public of forums. In Montana history, no one exemplified this philosophy more than *Helena Independent* editor Will Campbell, the state's most infamous poison pen editor. After nearly a century, his legacy still generates debate, condemnation, and outrage.

Will Campbell expanded the *Independent* from a small Democratic daily into one of the most politically important Montana newspapers of the early twentieth century. He did it, however, by infusing the paper with his own extremist opinions and by viciously attacking those who disagreed with him, the Democratic party, and the Anaconda Copper Mining Company. He reached his editorial zenith from 1917 to 1921—during the tumultuous years of World War I and the Red Scare of the early 1920s. For Campbell the Great War was not just a crusade against an oppressive overseas monarchy; it was also an opportunity to silence radicals, seditionists, socialists, anarchists, Marxists, Bolsheviks, and other politically dubious individuals at home. He used the wartime fears generated in the United States to promote bigotry and extremism and condone political housecleaning. He was a demagogue in the worst sense of the term—an early-twentieth-century version of Joseph McCarthy, who attacked those who did not agree with his narrow view of what a democracy should be—a well-ordered Anglo-Saxon society free from political debate and discord.

Born in 1881, Campbell attended the University of Nebraska, where he was employed as an editorial writer for the *Nebraska State Journal* in the late 1890s. From 1900 until 1909 he worked on a variety of newspapers including the *Denver Post,* where he developed his loathing of labor unions when he mediated an end to a particularly ugly strike against the paper. For several years he was employed by the Great Northern Railway in its publicity department, luring homesteaders onto the northern Great Plains with promises of abundant rainfall and bumper crops. It was while employed by the Great Northern that he acquired his love for Montana.

In early 1913 a group of Helena Democrats backed by the Anaconda Copper Mining Company purchased the *Independent* from publisher John S. M. Neill. The new owners soon hired Campbell as publisher and editor of the newspaper. Although labeled a Woodrow Wilson Democrat, Campbell never really displayed the Progressive political ideology that characterized that presidency. Like Wilson, however, Campbell was intolerant of other political philosophies and disliked what he called "hyphenated" Americans. Arch-Progressive Theodore Roosevelt called Wilson an "utterly selfish and cold-blooded politician, " a description that also applied to Campbell. He quickly worked his way up the Democratic hierarchy in Helena and became a close friend of Governor Sam Stewart. In his first issue as editor, on March 6, 1913, Campbell published a statement of purpose for the newspaper, writing:

> The first thing the *Helena Independent* will look for is news, not one-sided, prejudiced, tainted nor lacking. It is quite essential to be fair and give all the news as to be truthful editorially, as the greatest untruth may be conveyed to readers.

The Industrial Revolution in the United States began in 1865 and ended at the conclusion of World War I. During that fifty-year period, America experienced profound changes that eventually led to its emergence as a world power. Among them was the tremendous number of European immigrants who came to this country seeking a better life for themselves and their families. The migration was not especially popular with middle-class Americans, who saw them not as a cheap source of labor but as a threat to the status quo. They believed many immigrants from eastern and southern Europe brought radical political ideas with them that potentially threatened the country. It could be argued that the violent reactions to the labor strikes of the late nineteenth century were more out of fear of radicalism than they were of the concessions many of the workers wanted. Hyphenated Americans, as they were known to nativists, provided an easy target for many middle-class Americans, who felt they were politically unreliable and disloyal. The European War only seemed to intensify fears that had been brewing in America since the late 1860s. Campbell felt that the melting pot idea was overworked and did not reflect reality: "There is room for the right sort of immigrant in America but it is the height of folly to turn them loose in the cities of the more thickly populated sections of the country, where they enter into competition with American labor and cause such trouble as is observed, for instance, in the mining camps."

He aggressively supported immigration restrictions, especially for Germans, Italians, Russians and other eastern Europeans. He later stated, "He is no true American who in this crisis will discriminate between blood—who will unduly suspect or discourteously jeer any other American of any extraction whatsoever." To paraphrase Harry Truman, Campbell was good at "talking out of both sides of his mouth at the same time and lying out of both sides."

When the United States declared war on Germany in April 1917, Campbell was quick to jump on the pro-war, anti-German bandwagon. Although Germany was not a military threat to Montana, it did not deter Campbell from finding Huns ready to strike everywhere in the Treasure State—especially at Butte and Helena. On the front pages of his newspaper appeared stories suggesting that German airplanes regularly circled over the capitol city and that German saboteurs lurked in the mountains waiting for the opportunity to strike. Much of this reporting was based on rumor or was pure fabrication designed to stir up support for the war. What Campbell's stories also did was increase tension at home by preying on Montanans' fears about becoming embroiled in what many perceived to be an internal European problem. The problem was aggravated by a labor strike in Butte in 1917 that was supported by the radical Industrial Workers of the World (IWW), a Marxist organization that inspired dread among many Americans by openly advocating violence against Big Business. By late July 1917,

Will Campbell.

Campbell turned his attention away from German saboteurs and focused on the IWW.

Campbell's hatred of the IWW was first voiced in the pages of the *Independent* in 1914, when he reported that a "murderous band" of Wobblies had invaded the state. He even quoted railroad officials, who stated that they had sighted an army of 1,500 heavily armed IWWs headed for Butte. He felt, however, that Montana's climate might work to the state's advantage: "An IWW hates cold weather as badly as he despises a bath." Campbell accused the Wobblies of being traitors and, in one instance, suggested that a mass execution of them would solve most of the country's problems. When masked men lynched IWW organizer Frank Little in August, Campbell editorialized, "Good work: Let them continue to hang every IWW in the state." Although the murder was anything but a vigilante-type action, he praised the killers by comparing them to Montana's pioneer vigilance committees: "It sort of quickens the blood in the veins of some pioneers of Helena to see the fatal figures in print—3–7–77." In late 1917 he made calls for a special session of the legislature to enact antisedition legislation because, he felt, the Little murder would inspire traitorous talk and revenge killings by the IWW. Campbell had no sympathy for those who opposed the war or appeared to be dragging their feet in support of it.

In March 1917 Governor Sam Stewart appointed Campbell to serve on the Montana Council of Defense. The Council was formed at the request of the Wilson Administration to spread propaganda, motivate military enlistment, and promote the sale of Liberty Bonds and contributions to the Red Cross. It was also responsible for supporting the formation of local "Liberty Leagues" and inspiring patriotism for the war effort. Because the Council's meetings were held in secret and Campbell was the only journalist on it, the *Independent* was the only way information about its activities were disseminated. With the passage of the Anti-Sedition Act in 1918, the Council became responsible for the enactment of the new law. The act made it illegal to say or do anything that could be perceived as hindering the war effort or as treason. In effect, the law abrogated Americans' First Amendment rights. Campbell, who professed a deep love of American democracy, publicly ridiculed those who expressed concern over the government's violation of those rights.

Through Campbell, the *Independent* became the mouthpiece of the Council. His attacks on seditionists, traitors, slackers, immigrants, and radical unions grew bolder and more noxious in 1918. His connection to the Anaconda Copper Mining Company and its policies became so obvious that Attorney General Burton K. Wheeler stated that the "*Independent* was absolutely subsidized and subservient to the mining interests of the state." Indeed, even after the Armistice in 1918, Campbell continued his attacks on labor, labeling them agents of Bolshevism and paving the way for the Red Scare in Montana in the early 1920s.

It was mainly through Campbell's efforts that the Council passed its notorious Order #3, banning the use of the German language in Montana, which he called the most "despised language in history." The order caused Fred Naegele's German-language newspaper, the *Staats-Zeitung,* to cease publication and precipitated a bitter feud between the two men that called into question Naegele's loyalty. Although the Council's mission had begun altruistically enough, by 1918 it had become an entirely different agency "used to harass political opponents and attack individuals and organizations that opposed the war or did not back it as fervently as they did." Campbell believed in nothing short of an "ignominious death for traitors." He also aggressively supported deportation laws for Americans deemed disloyal: "Then when one of these blat-mouths, these un-American individuals who sympathize with Prussian murderers of women and children, started spewing his sedition or acting it, it would an excellent thing if he or she were escorted down to the sea shore or to the border and kicked out of the country never to return."

When the fighting ended in November 1918, Campbell and the Council turned its attention to a new threat—Communism. Campbell equated the Russian Bolsheviks with the IWW. He especially despised "Armchair Bolsheviks, Rocking Chair pinks who are a class composed largely of neurotic men and women of wealth who have nothing better to do."

Surprisingly, considering his aversion to opposing political ideas and his basically isolationist stance, Campbell supported Wilson's League of Nations proposal. He used the *Independent* to publicly castigate Republicans who opposed Wilson's Fourteen Points. Like his idol, Woodrow Wilson, Campbell detested those who disagreed with him, believing them stupid and uninformed. In 1920 he helped elect a progressive Republican, Joseph Dixon, to the governor's office. Dixon was opposed by Democrat Burton K. Wheeler, a man Campbell hated and often ridiculed in the *Independent.*

But Campbell's support was short-lived. Eventually Campbell

turned on Dixon when the governor accused Montana State Penitentiary warden Frank Conley of corruption. A virulent anti–Anaconda Copper Mining Company crusader, Dixon accused Conley, who enjoyed the support of the company (and, therefore, the *Independent*), of stealing $200,000 in state funds and state-owned equipment. Although he had an annual wage of only $4,000, Conley had managed to accumulate a fortune worth $500,000—a fact that had drawn the attention of Dixon. Campbell actively supported Conley and attacked what he perceived was Dixon's financial mismanagement, even when it was proved that Dixon had saved the state a considerable amount of money. Although Campbell claimed the *Independent* would support the ideals of progressive reform in 1913 and reiterated it in 1917, by 1921 the newspaper was contributing to the demise of the reform movement in Montana.

Campbell attacked what he said was Dixon's reckless spending when he allegedly bought a $12.50 gravy boat with state funds for the governor's mansion. Although it was later revealed that the gravy boat was, in fact, part of a set of dishes ordered by Campbell's friend and fellow Council of Defense member Sam Stewart when he was still in office, it made no difference to the venomous editor.

In March 1924 Campbell rashly accused Helena's competing newspaper, the *Record-Herald,* of defrauding the state for the publication of the state treasurer's report. Campbell charged that the rival newspaper's managers reached "their hands into the treasury and with false affidavits extract[ed] $11,685 more from the state than they are charging the County of Lewis and Clark for the same services. Of all the open-faced hypocrites, the *Record-Herald* is the indecent limit." In the weeks following this accusation, Campbell charged the Dixon administration of collaborating with the publisher of the *Record-Herald* to keep Campbell's auditors from examining the paper's financial records. For Campbell, his competitor's supposed indiscretion abetted by Dixon was proof that the governor was hopelessly corrupt.

In fact, *Record-Herald* editor Charles Reifenrath stated that the price they charged the State to print the report was the same price that Campbell's *Independent* had charged before losing the contract when Dixon was elected in 1920. Indeed, the publishing costs were set by the 1889 state constitution. Reifenrath reported:

> Everybody knows that [Campbell's] hatred is traced to the fact that Governor Dixon wants the tax dodgers to pay their

just taxes and that the tax dodgers keep the *Independent* alive . . . In our opinion the *Helena Independent* would steal anything, alter claims, lie, perjure itself, or commit any crime or transgression to do the state administration harm, gratify its hate, and serve its masters, and we believe its record is proof of the soundness of this view. . . . When lies and perjury are daily output of a newspaper it is not surprising the owner should be barred from the state auditor's vaults. Bootleg whiskey, free love and reform school antecedents do not make for a character that respects the law. Crime is natural to such a genesis and a habit of life.

Shortly after this condemnation, Campbell shifted his rhetoric away from the *Record-Herald* and directed it specifically at Dixon.

By all accounts a workaholic, Campbell went to work each day as early as 5:00 A.M., sometimes not leaving his office until after midnight. Although he had a wide circle of acquaintances, he maintained no close friendships because of his dedication to the newspaper. Perhaps because Dixon was right in his accusations, the Anaconda Copper Mining Company instructed its editors to tone down their rhetoric in the company-owned newspapers in the mid-1920s. It was only after the Anaconda Copper Mining Company pulled Campbell's fangs that the *Independent* became a respected newspaper and the editorials boring.

In late 1937 Will Campbell stepped away from the editor's desk of the *Independent*. His health broken by his punishing work schedule, he retired and moved to Kirkland, Washington, with his wife and died of heart disease in December 1938. Pallbearers at his funeral in Helena included Sam Stewart and Frank Conley.

The legacy of the *Independent* during the Campbell years is one of hatred and intolerance. He was a virulent nativist who distrusted foreigners and condemned any political ideas different from his own. Because of his activities, many people who questioned the war or had the temerity to question Campbell were brutalized in the press, some even going to prison for sedition. He fabricated stories and passed them off as true to support his narrow and extremist views. People like Will Campbell made a difficult time in America's history more complex and a lot darker. Historian Charles Sackett Johnson wrote that Campbell was a "talented man overtaken, like the nation, by an obsessive hysteria. Instead of using his influential newspaper to set the country he loved straight, Campbell was at the forefront of the movement to strip away rights that were guaranteed in the Constitution he venerated."

It can be argued that Campbell's one redeeming grace was his love for the state of Montana—a love he passed on to his only son, the compiler of two volumes of the once-definitive Helena history, *From the Quarries of Last Chance Gulch*. Will Campbell's affection for the state withers, however, when measured against his vitriolic writing and extremism, which made Montana a much more intolerant place to live during a difficult period in the state's history.

~

Sources

Much has been written about Will Campbell over the past twenty years as historians delve deeper into Montana's more recent history. Campbell's writings and actions were so abhorrent to contemporary historians, however, that it is difficult to find an objective source on the man's career (this historian included). The best source of information is Will Campbell himself in the pages of the *Helena Independent* from 1913 until his retirement in 1937. Another good source of information about Campbell is the Montana Council of Defense records at the Montana Historical Society in Helena. For good overviews of Montana during World War I, Michael Malone, Richard Roeder, and William Lang's *Montana: A History of Two Centuries* (rev. ed., University of Washington, 1991) and Arnon Gutfeld's *Montana's Agony: Years of War and Hysteria, 1917–1921* (University of Florida, 1979) provide information about that chaotic time in the state's history.

John X. Beidler: Vigilante, Executioner, and Pint-Size Bully

Jon Axline

Forestvale Cemetery is the final resting place for John X. Beidler, one of Montana's most well-known pioneer lawmen and vigilantes. Referred to popularly as "X," Beidler claimed to have been involved in most of the pivotal events that defined frontier Montana. Many of his contemporaries glorified him as fearless, honest, trustworthy, and "indifferent under the most trying circumstances." Others described Beidler as a liar, braggart, and pint-size bully. Beidler was, in fact, all these things.

Despite his many-layered personality, Beidler was primarily known as a vigilante. He boasted that he had pursued and executed "thirty men of the Plummer Gang" and had also supervised several hangings in Helena. Although long a deputy U.S. marshal, he was also a customs collector, assistant Indian agent, and Wells Fargo messenger. Beidler also claimed to have been present when John Johnston received the nickname of "Liver-Eatin'" and supposedly aided "Portugee" Phillips in his epic ride to Fort Laramie with news of the Fetterman Massacre in 1866. Although an admirer of the Indians, his actions toward them were often brutal and lacking in any compassion.

Beidler stood about 5 foot 6 inches tall and often dressed in clothes that appeared to be too big for him. In many photographs he is shown brandishing a shotgun that was several inches longer than he was tall. Beidler was also short on patience. In his autobiography he said that any delays were apt to make him become "boiling, you bet, and indignant into the bargain." One of his less savory traits seems to have been a tendency to take things (including clothing) from corpses for his personal use.

Born in Pennsylvania in 1832, Beidler was one of twelve children born to John and Anna Beidler. According to his younger brother, Beidler received his middle initial as a nickname. In order to distinguish his clothes from those of his brothers, he marked them with a large "X." The "X," therefore, stood for neither "Xavier" nor "Xelpho" as has been generally reported. After working for a time as a cobbler, broom maker, and brick maker, Beidler left Pennsylvania for Illinois, where he unsuccessfully tried farming and later, he claimed, fought side by side with abolitionist John Brown in Kansas. Beidler was in Colorado in 1859 and then drifted on to Alder Gulch in Montana after gold was discovered there in 1863.

For a time Beidler worked as a placer miner before directing his efforts to trading in much-needed supplies for the mining camps. Events in Virginia City and Bannack, however, caused Beidler to "quit prospecting for gold and [begin to] prospect for human fiends." Beidler won his place in Montana history as the eager executioner of Henry Plummer's road agent gang, which was then allegedly terrorizing the Montana mining camps. Beidler is reportedly responsible for two of the most famous (or infamous) vigilante quotes during the winter of 1863–1864. When George Ives asked Wilbur Fisk Sanders for more time to write his mother and sister, Beidler, who was guarding the prisoner, shouted, "Sanders, ask him how much time he gave the Dutchman!" Also, when asked if he felt anything when he hanged road agent Jack Gallagher, Beidler is said to have replied, "Yes, I felt for his left ear!"

In late spring of 1864, Beidler worked for a time as a Wells Fargo messenger before becoming a deputy U.S. marshal under A. C. Botkin. By 1865 he was a regular visitor to Last Chance Gulch, where he claimed to have organized the Helena vigilantes to "try" to execute John Keene—Helena's first murderer. Beidler's claim, however, is unsubstantiated. As was often the case, Beidler claimed a major role in this event, but nowhere is he mentioned in contemporary accounts of the Keene murder case.

An "outlander" and member of the "criminal class," John Keene ambushed and killed Henry Slater at a Helena saloon on June 17, 1865. After his capture, Keene was tried by the vigilante "court" and sentenced to hang, although he maintained that Slater would have killed him if he had had the chance (Slater was napping when Keene shot him). Keene was the first to hang from the tree on Dry Gulch. Beidler claimed to have organized the Helena vigilance committee and to have acted as Keene's executioner. If true, he did this as a duly deputized law enforcement officer. Regardless, Beidler is not seen as a stellar individual—he is guilty either of self-aggrandizement or of placing the law of vigilance committee and the rope over the established judicial system.

John X. Beidler.

Photograph by Keller, Helena, Montana. Montana Historical Society, Helena.

The Keene case was only one in a series of events that reveal Beidler's penchant for standing firmly . . . on which ever side of the legal fence was most convenient for him. In 1867 Beidler's friend and fellow vigilante, Nathaniel Langford, described Helena as "infested with thieves, ruffians and murderers. Shooting affrays, resulting in death . . . had been of almost daily occurrence." In this town of bad characters, Beidler found plenty of work. In one case Beidler became embroiled in the cold-blooded murder of a black man on Election Day—the first election in which blacks were empowered to vote. Although the U.S. Congress had granted blacks the right to vote, the Montana territorial legislature denied them that right. Acting on orders from U.S. Marshal Botkin, Beidler was detailed to safeguard the polling places for the country's newest enfranchised citizens. During Beidler's watch a janitor named Sammy, who ironically had not yet decided whether he would vote, was killed by a bigoted muleskinner named Leach. Showing an amazing amount of grit, Beidler braved a human wall of armed roughs to arrest Leach and took the man to jail. Leach later escaped and was not pursued for punishment.

In 1870, however, Beidler's vigilante sympathies almost got him arrested for murder. In January a Chinese miner named Ah Chow killed John Retzer in Helena. After a short chase, Deputy U.S. Marshal Beidler captured the man, returned him to Helena, and then turned him over to the "vigilantes." Ah Chow was hanged and a placard pinned to him that stated, BEWARE! THE VIGILANTES STILL LIVE! Beidler then had the audacity to apply for and receive the bounty offered for the capture of Ah Chow. The editor of the *Deer Lodge Independent* criticized Beidler: "We could not believe that any mere private citizens would engage in so lawless a proceeding and then have the temerity to acknowledge his guilt by applying for and receiving the reward." The hanging spawned a short-lived and, Beidler claimed, desperado-led antivigilante movement in Helena. He allegedly received a note warning, "We . . . will give you no more time to prepare for death than the many men you have murdered. . . . We shall live to see you buried beside the poor Chinaman you murdered."

Except for a brief stint as a Yellowstone National Park guide and assistant Indian agent, Beidler continued to serve as deputy U.S. marshal in Montana Territory throughout the 1870s and into the 1880s. By 1888, however, his health failed and he lived largely on the charity of friends and the income derived from telling stories at local Helena watering holes. Beidler's exploits became more colorful with each telling, with him a major player in almost all the major events of Montana's early history. It would seem the more frequent the libations, the more daring and colorful the tales became.

Just before his death, Beidler had a number of photographs taken that showed him in Western garb toting a large rifle or shotgun. Although he hoped to sell the photos for much-needed cash, Beidler ended up giving most of them away to his friends around Helena. Troubled by insomnia, Beidler wandered the streets of Helena at night and drank in the saloons until he could fall asleep.

Despite his often questionable character, Beidler was a man with friends in high places. In February 1889 Lee Mantle of Butte introduced a resolution in the last territorial legislature to provide for the relief of Beidler. The resolution failed by a vote of twelve to seven. The *Helena Independent* lamented, "Indeed it seems that this general ignorance of the great work done by the most celebrated character of the frontier times . . . resulted in defeating the measure." The defeated measure reveals Montana's growing discomfort with its own "wild past."

On January 22, 1890, a destitute Beidler died in his room at the Pacific Hotel from complications resulting from pneumonia. Upon his death, City Marshal C. D. Hard and Street Commissioner L. F. Evans formed a committee to raise money to pay for Beidler's funeral. The funeral was held in the Ming Opera House and attended by hundreds of Beidler's friends and associates. Wilbur Fisk Sanders gave the eulogy for his old friend, who was buried in the city cemetery on Benton Avenue.

His obituary mourned that his death removed "the last conspicuous figure in a notable class of pioneers. The spirit of adventure and not the greed of gold brought him to an almost unknown and lawless section of the country—when rugged honesty and dauntless courage were needed to purge the territory of desperadoes, he became a leader among fearless men."

In 1903 the Montana Society of Pioneers exhumed the body and moved Beidler's remains to the more picturesque Forestvale Cemetery in the Helena Valley. They also raised a "great rough boulder, emblematic of his rugged character" over his new resting place. Donated by Kain Granite Works, the stone is inscribed "John X. Beidler; Born August 14, 1831; Died Jan. 22, 1890; 3–7–77; Public Benefactor, Brave Pioneer, To True Occasion." The Society of Pioneers conveniently forgot or ignored Beidler's less-than-savory characteristics when it erected that rough-hewn monument. While a firm believer in justice, this self-described "terror to roughs" ignored the law and delighted in his reputation as the vigilante executioner of some of Montana's earliest desperados.

~

Sources

The amount of historical material available about John X. Beidler is staggering. He was everywhere at once and was, apparently, everybody's friend. The best sources about Beidler's early career in Montana are Thomas Dimsdale's *Vigilantes of Montana* and Nathaniel P. Langford's *Vigilante Days and Ways*. Both volumes are apologias for the vigilantes' actions during the early 1860s. Both make much of Beidler's role in the executions of Henry Plummer's gang but also provide a picture of the hangman that is, at times, not very flattering. There are also frequent references to Beidler in memoirs written about Montana's territorial days and, in the twentieth century, frequent articles in Montana newspapers. Most portray a man dedicated to law and order, but an occasional negative depiction portrays Beidler more as a scoundrel or social outsider than a frontier hero. Beidler's association with Liver-Eatin' Johnston (described elsewhere in this book) is also of questionable veracity. The newspaper clippings are located in the vertical files at the Montana Historical Society.

One of the most interesting accounts of Beidler's life is his autobiography. Published in 1957 by the University of Oklahoma Press, *X. Beidler, Vigilante* was edited by Helena Fitzgerald Sanders, the daughter-in-law of Beidler's longtime friend, Wilbur Fisk Sanders. The autobiography provides an interesting insight into Beidler's life and a justification for his relishing his role as hangman in early Montana history.

THE SECRETS AND LIES OF MARY ANN ECKERT
Ellen Baumler

HELENA GROCER JOHN DENN HAD JUST CRAWLED INTO BED AND WAS ABOUT to wind his pocket watch, as was his habit before putting out the lamp, when he heard a rap at the back door. He carefully turned back the bedclothes, put on his carpet slippers, and answered the knock in his nightshirt and drawers. It was not particularly unusual for Denn to receive customers he knew after-hours at his back door. The visitor wanted a bottle of whiskey, so Denn took up a candle, a funnel, and a bottle and went down to the cellar to draw it from the cask. As he bent down to open the spigot, the intruder hit him once on top of the head with a hammerlike weapon, punching a fatal hole in his skull. As Denn fell to the floor, the murderer dealt two more blows for good measure—one above each eye. On the way out, the killer returned to the store, went through Denn's pockets and emptied his purse, and then vanished into the night. Denn lay in the cellar for some hours in a spreading puddle of gore. Customers made the grisly discovery the following morning, October 28, 1879, when he failed to open the store. During investigation of the crime scene, passersby on the street peered through the barred cellar windows, where the body was readily visible, lying before the liquor barrel. The Helena *Independent* reported: "The eyes were closed and the face of the dead would have worn an expression of deep, calm slumber but for the tightly compressed lips, around which seemed to play a sad and bitter smile."

Denn was known to have perhaps as much as $3,000 cash in his safe. He was also fond of sampling his liquid inventory and when "in his cups" would sometimes talk freely about how much money he kept on hand. He had been heard to say a few days before his murder that he had nearly $10,000 hidden in his wine cellar. Attorney John Shober, who was a neighbor and longtime acquaintance of Denn's, found nearly $7,000 in cash and securities, missed by the intruder, hidden in a tin box in the cellar while police searched the premises. What business Shober had at Denn's during the investigation of the crime scene was never questioned. Denn's safe, however, was found empty of the gold coins the victim's brother-in-law had seen there a few days previous. The key, which Denn always kept on his person, never surfaced. Despite an astounding $12,000 reward and several arrests in the case, no one was formally charged. But there was plenty of suspicion. Folks in Helena whispered about their neighbors and speculated about who knew more than they were willing to tell.

On March 5, 1884, John A. Jessrang was lynched by a mob at Dillon. Jessrang had been proprietor of a butcher shop at the time of Denn's murder and had been among those questioned. Jessrang was in the Beaverhead County Jail, indicted in the murder of V. H. Johnson. The motive was the small pocket change in Johnson's pocket. It was an especially repugnant crime because Jessrang attacked Johnson from behind in cold blood and then attempted to burn the corpse. After burying the charred remains in a snowbank, Jessrang stumbled into the small mining camp of Dewey along the Big Hole River, his feet painfully frozen. A passerby along the trail found the burned body, and Jessrang was arrested and indicted. He was being detained at the county jail awaiting trial and recovering from the amputation of both feet. When more of Johnson's remains were discovered and brought to town for public display, citizens became impatient. A mob of some fifteen vigilantes broke into the jail. As they strung him up, the men questioned Jessrang repeatedly, urging him to come clean. He never gave any indication that he had a part in the crime against Denn, but the heinous nature of Johnson's murder brought back all-too-recent memories of Denn's gruesome end. Uneasy Helenans again began to lock their doors. For years after Denn's untimely death, detectives followed leads and shadowed suspects, but the pieces to the puzzle never fit. Who killed John Denn remained a dark mystery.

Nearly a decade after Denn's demise in spring 1888, longtime Helena photographer Mrs. Mary Ann Eckert lay ill with a terminal heart condition. Sarah Holmes, a professional nurse and self-proclaimed friend, cared for Mrs. Eckert in the weeks before her death on May 3. A week later, rumors began to surface that the photographer had confided some spectacular information to Mrs. Holmes. After hints to the authorities, Mrs. Holmes finally revealed what the sick woman had supposedly told her. Mrs. Eckert's deathbed revelation, reported in detailed installments in both the *Independent* and the *Herald* between May 10 and 17, 1888, left Helena reeling. The crux of it was that Mary Ann Eckert had confessed to the murder of John Denn. Mrs. Holmes claimed that Mrs. Eckert said, "I went in the night to Denn, called him up, took a bottle. I went in the cellar with him and hit him a lick. I killed John Denn with a hatchet." Among the several discrepancies in the confession was the fact that Denn had actually been killed with a specialized hammer, like that used in shoeing horses, not a hatchet. He had also been hit with more than one "lick." Mrs. Holmes told minute details of the alleged confession, and she also knew intimate details of Mrs. Eckert's life. She also claimed that Mrs. Eckert told her that the murder weapon was still in use in the Eckert household. Over the course of the next two weeks, both Helena newspapers interviewed, questioned, and speculated. Among those questioned were Nurse Holmes; the dead woman's daughter, Jessie Schwabe; acquaintances; old-timers; and people on the street. Some believed the confession; others did not. Everyone agreed, however, that Mrs. Eckert had been peculiar and eccentric. Her daughter, Jessie, blamed her mother's behavior on an assault a few years previous. During that incident, Mrs. Eckert had been hit with a hatchet and had not seemed quite right ever since. Jessie did not volunteer further details.

Friends agreed that for some years before her death, Mrs. Eckert had been, as one described it, "possessed of vague forebodings," saying often to her friends that she was undergoing the greatest mental tortures due only to the damned. She seemed obsessed with the Denn murder. One acquaintance told the *Weekly Herald* that early one morning in the summer of 1878 he encountered Mrs. Eckert at the corner where Denn's grocery used to be. Workmen were excavating for a new building on the site of the cellar where Denn was murdered. Mrs. Eckert looked pale as death, her pallor ghastly, and her hair was disheveled. She seemed greatly troubled. He asked her what she was doing up so early. Mrs. Eckert was slow to reply but finally turned her eyes toward the cellar, raised her arm, and pointed a shaky finger at the gaping hole. In a chilling voice she replied, "I am watching that accursed spot."

After the alleged confession was out, authorities scrambled to find waybills and receipts that would prove, or disprove, Mrs. Eckert's whereabouts on the night of October 27, 1879. Her family claimed that she had gone to Virginia City to open a studio there. Stageline receipts showed that Mrs. Eckert had purchased a $15 ticket, departed Helena on October 12, and returned the following February. While the *Independent* maintained that the waybills proved conclusively that Mrs. Eckert was in Virginia City when Denn was murdered, the *Herald* insisted that the dates proved nothing. Some witnesses claimed to have seen Mrs. Eckert in Virginia City, while others were certain they had seen her milling around with the crowd the very morning after the murder.

Mrs. Eckert's photographic studio in Helena was on South Main Street from at least 1868, and she was considered a talented artist and a shrewd businesswoman. She was haughty in her professional claims, advertising in the Helena City Directory of 1868: "Those desirous of obtaining a facsimile of their features should embrace the first favorable opportunity for a 'sitting' . . . and if their picture is not a lovely one, it will be owing entirely to the fact that, the original is not a beauty—and not be attributed to the camera, or any lack of skill in the artist." She kept up with her profession, employing the most up-to-date techniques.

Madame, as she liked to call herself, early on seemed to have an interest in the gruesome. It was she who took the famous photograph of the double hanging of Joseph Wilson and Arthur Compton in Helena in 1870. Madame Eckert was a keen businesswoman who knew very well how to protect her assets. R. G. Dun and Company, arbiters of financial reputation, had guardedly recommended her business because she paid her bills promptly and she was professionally skilled but noted that Mrs. Eckert had a rather unsavory reputation, associated with the characters of the frontier underworld, and by choice had always maintained her business and her residence on the fringe of the red-light district. Lengthy discussions in the Helena newspapers weighing Mrs. Eckert's guilt or innocence thoroughly bear out these questionable associations. Both the *Helena Independent* and the *Herald* pointedly refer to numerous scandals but decline to elaborate. Rather, these reports take for granted that readers are aware of the gossip: that Mrs. Eckert began her Helena career as a hurdy-gurdy dancer; that she went to Virginia City to care for a man who had been shot; that she had a long-standing liaison with a prominent, and very jealous, Helena man; and that she had swindled the husband with whom she had emigrated to Montana Territory in 1866. The 1870 federal census places Mrs. Eckert in the category widowed/divorced, but court records prove that divorce papers were not even filed until 1873. These show that Mrs. Eckert charged her husband, John S. Eckert, with abandonment and petitioned the court to waive legal fees because she was too poor to pay. Yet she took her daughter on a trip to Paris and paid for her to study there. Mrs. Eckert's divorce from John was never finalized. In the 1880 census, Mrs. Eckert

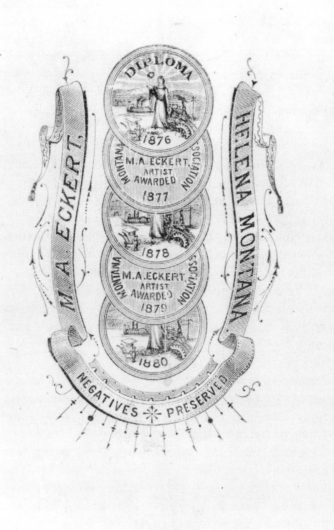

Mary Ann Eckert's professional crest found on reverse side of portraits.
MONTANA HISTORICAL SOCIETY, HELENA.

subtracted substantial years from her true age and passed herself off as a widow knowing full well the whereabouts of her absent husband. Indications are that he may not have abandoned her at all but more likely in the end fled from her clutches. In the weeks before her death, Mrs. Eckert made a detailed will dividing her substantial estate. She remembered John, leaving him the sum of one dollar.

Probate records reveal that Mary Ann Eckert was worth a small fortune. She owned a total of nine houses and buildings in Helena. These and the contents therein totaled nearly $25,000 at the time of her death. Fire insurance maps clearly show that two of Mrs. Eckert's properties—one where she herself resided and did business until her illness—were on Wood Street in the very heart of Helena's red-light district. The services she offered, besides photography, included instruction on the piano and guitar, painting and drawing lessons, and rented rooms. A list of rents collected after her death for the month of May 1888 contains nearly fifty anonymous entries. Why were these anonymous, and why were there so many? Mrs. Eckert was very likely trafficking in the skin trade and renting rooms for illicit purposes, if not managing some of the women. Probate records also include a list of Mrs. Eckert's outstanding debts. The first item and largest amount, for $637.56, she owed to John Shober, who found the overlooked moneybox at the scene of the Denn murder. In a strange twist, that loan with interest had just come due a few days before her death. Mrs. Eckert was a woman who promptly repaid her debts. She knew she was going to die. Why would she settle her other business and make her will but leave this one loan outstanding?

Deputy U. S. Marshall Quirk told *Herald* reporters that he had questioned Mrs. Eckert about Denn on several occasions. He found her behavior eccentric and disturbing. The deputy told *Herald* reporters that a very distraught Mrs. Eckert had repeatedly come to his house late at night to accuse attorney John Shober of trying to kill her. She also repeatedly tried to pin the Denn murder on Shober. When Marshall Quirk told Shober of Mrs. Eckert's accusations, Shober became very agitated and said that she had better keep her damned mouth shut or he would run her out of town. On several occasions Mrs. Eckert vehemently expressed her hatred toward Shober in public; Shober expressed like sentiments toward her. Shober even once physically assaulted Mrs. Eckert. Could this have been the hatchet incident? Why would this prominent attorney become so upset over a crazy woman's demented rantings? Mrs. Eckert clearly knew something about the Denn case that Shober did not want revealed. It is odd that she, having a fairly good income, would borrow money from a man she detested. Perhaps Shober made the loan to Mrs. Eckert to keep her quiet. According to court documents, a year after Mrs. Eckert's death Shober petitioned for repayment of the loan with interest. The court denied payment.

John Shober's name comes up repeatedly in discussions of Mrs. Eckert and the Denn murder, but, as far as records show, the authorities never questioned him. Shober was a pioneer attorney and a member of the elite circle of territorial lawyers who laid the cornerstones of the state's judicial system. His stellar career in Montana Territory began in 1864 when Shober defeated Cornelius Hedges—his lifelong friend—in the first local election for district attorney. He earned an enviable reputation as a gifted trial lawyer. Neither the *Independent* nor the *Herald* would dare besmirch the name of such a prominent man. However, the mere mention of Shober in connection with this case makes it all the more sensational. Both newspapers pointedly refer to Shober with underlying accusations. It doesn't take much to read between the lines.

At the time of the murder, Shober's discovery of the missing moneybox in Denn's cellar is odd indeed, and the *Daily Herald*'s description at the time is equally strange. Describing the attorney's flamboyant emergence with the moneybox and $7,000 intact, the reporter wrote, "Mr. Shober's beaming countenance appeared from the wine cellar." Even though he made the discovery, why would Shober be "beaming" at a gruesome crime scene, with the body of his neighbor lying there in the cellar hardly cold? Two weeks after Denn's death, the *Independent* cryptically reported that Shober had gone to Bozeman on business. "Since his new departure his many friends are glad to observe that he is looking more like himself than he has done for years." Something clearly had been bothering Shober. These and other innuendoes in the press seem to indicate that Shober's suspected involvement in the Denn murder was much more than casual.

Shober, Denn, and Mrs. Eckert had known one another since mining camp days. Denn had frequently loaned money to the women of the tenderloin and to Mary Ann Eckert as well. Both men were bachelors. Perhaps there was more than money involved, and one of the men was Mrs. Eckert's "jealous" friend. The answers to these questions, unfortunately, can be nothing more than speculation.

The main question regarding Mrs. Eckert, however, is whether she actually confessed to the Denn murder, and, if she did, was she telling the truth? Some believed Mrs. Holmes was paid to tell the story in order to put the crime permanently to rest. Most folks and the newspapers, however, finally concluded that Mrs. Eckert's confession was contrived but that it was made to protect someone more guilty than she was herself. All were convinced that she knew more than she told and that she shared in the blood money—the $3,000 missing from Denn's safe.

Lest the accusation of Shober be too hasty, it is expedient to note that there were others who appeared guilty. After Mrs. Holmes's story was out, an unnamed attorney related a strange incident. A man came into his office claiming that his business partner had committed the crime. The attorney recalled that the man had "a wild, haunted look . . . and he seemed to be suffering from some heavy, mental burden." The man told how he had gone to bed exhausted: "How long I slept I cannot say, but was suddenly aroused by an icy breath that chilled me through and through: starting up and who should I see standing there natural as life, with the great holes in his forehead, but John Denn. . . . A moment later the spirit in a piteous, pleading tone exclaimed, 'You know the murderer. Hand him over that I may sleep in peace.'" The phantom then slowly faded.

The attorney notified authorities, but the accused person had fled. According to the *Weekly Independent,* the frightened snitch was later judged insane and sent to an asylum.

If John Shober had some part in the Denn murder, it must have shadowed him for a very long time. He lived to a ripe old age and died in 1925 at ninety-three. The brick home he long shared with his niece Hattie and her husband, attorney C. B. Nolan, still stands—despite recent threats to tear it down for parking—next to the old St. Paul's Methodist Church at Lawrence and Warren Streets. What tales its walls might tell.

Mrs. Holmes, whose integrity also came into serious question as the story unfolded, proved hungry for publicity—and no friend to the dying Mrs. Eckert, as she had claimed to be. No friend would have shared intimate details of Mrs. Eckert's life with the press, especially with the dead woman's family living in the same community. Both Shober and Holmes are worthy of some contempt.

As for the subject of this study, what of Mary Ann Eckert? Did she commit the crime and confess to it? This scenario seems highly unlikely. If she did confess, it was almost certainly a false confession. Putting

John Shober. Portrait by M. A. Eckert, Helena, Montana.

aside the nineteenth-century intrigue and innuendo by which Mary Ann Eckert's contemporaries judged her, and viewing her in a more objective light from the vantage point of time, she emerges as a product of the frontier's roughest edges.

Mrs. Eckert's deteriorated mental state, well documented by her friends, may make her seem a victim. But her mental tortures were brought about by her own actions. Without a doubt she had answers and could have fingered the true murderer. Instead, the secrets and lies that she took with her to the grave left a web so tangled that it defies unraveling. Thanks to Mrs. Eckert, the murder of John Denn may never be solved.

Likely, John Denn himself would have judged Mrs. Eckert without mercy for denying him justice. Mary Ann Eckert takes her place in Montana's Hall of Shame for that which she could have done but did not do: tell the truth. Among all the comments and remarks about her, not a single person spoke a kind word in her behalf, nor did anyone praise her for her pioneer work in photography. She was a rarity in the early community for her business acumen and her profession, and despite her shortcomings she was a talented artist. It is unfortunate that she has to be a "jerk" to be remembered—but then, well-behaved women rarely make history.

~

Sources

A few years ago when historian Paula Petrik was researching Helena women on the mining frontier for her book *No Step Backwards,* she came upon a sensational and complicated murder that occurred around Halloween in 1879. Central to the bizarre story was one Mary Ann Eckert, whose involvement in the case deepened the mystery. When Paula left Montana to teach at the University of Maine, she left some files behind with Lory Morrow, program manager at the Montana Historical Society's photograph archives. Among them was one containing preliminary research on this case, with the suggestion that sometime someone should investigate it further. Lory passed Paula's notes along to me, and I picked up the thread.

The Helena newspapers provide a wealth of information on the Denn case. Coverage by the *Helena Daily Herald* and *Daily Independent* begins with the discovery of the body on October 28, 1879, and follows the case in detail on October 29 and 30. Denn's obituary and funeral notice is covered on October 30. The Dillon *Tribune* details the murder of V. H. Johnson and the lynching of John A. Jessrang on March 10, 1883. Homer Faust re-creates the whole story in a Montana News Association Insert dated October 24, 1932.

All the Helena newspapers carried stories of the confession and periodic updates. Most informative are the *Helena Weekly Herald* of May 8 and the *Weekly Independent* of May 10, 1888. The *Weekly Independent* of May 17 recaps the events and interviews citizens, polling their opinions on the case.

The Lewis and Clark County Courthouse contains a trail of records related to Mary Ann Eckert. Tucked away in the vault are boxes of divorce proceedings, filed by year. The Eckert divorce papers are housed there. Most interesting, however, are the probate records from the Old Series, housed on microfilm, that include all the papers filed after Eckert's death. Included is the outstanding loan to John Shober, an inventory of Mrs. Eckert's nine Helena properties with their contents and values, and Eckert's will with the designation of Dr. William Steele as executor of her estate. These papers lend credence to the rather shady reputation that Mrs. Eckert had among her neighbors and contemporaries.

Mrs. Eckert advertised in the Helena city directories. The most extensive of her ads appears in 1868, quoted above in the text. The Montana Historical Society has some of Mrs. Eckert's photographs in its collection. Among these are the hanging of Compton and Wilson and a portrait of John Shober. The knowledge of the later history between the Eckert and Shober gives deeper meaning to the photograph.

Because of John Shober's prominence in the community, there are references and sketches of him scattered throughout the Montana Historical Society Library; a vertical file preserves some of these.

Another version of this story, with a focus on reported sightings of the ghost of John Denn, appears in my book *Spirit Tailings* (Montana Historical Society Press, 2002).

Wine, Women, and Whiz Wagons:
The Life and Crimes of Vera Prosser
Jodie Foley

THE DAWN OF THE TWENTIETH CENTURY USHERED IN YEARS OF PROMISE FOR American women. Advances in birth control, childbirth, and home cleaning technologies promised healthier and smaller families. Progressive Era reform movements promised the end of myriad social evils—from alcohol abuse to poverty to prostitution. And changes in cultural mores promised women the freedom to pursue higher education, join the workforce in increased numbers, and enter the political debate over public morality. These last promises became a reality for only a select few, but the fact that women expected more freedoms indicated a change in the previously accepted definition of womanhood.

In the nineteenth century a "True Woman" was described as innocent, physically weak, eager to please, and willing to accept suffering. By contrast, the early twentieth century's "New Woman" was educated and physically active—prompting the fashion change from corset to bloomers. She was vocal in her opinions and more likely to postpone marriage—or file for divorce. As divergent as these two definitions seem, they share the perception that women were morally superior to men. The Victorian woman brought her moral acumen to bear on the intimate family circle—teaching her children proper behavior, keeping an immaculate home, and creating a moral haven for her world-weary husband.

But there was a less altruistic side to the rise of the New Woman. Women stepped out of the family circle and into the public domain because they wanted to, and because changes in cultural mores provided the justification to do so. Most women used these new opportunities in a socially conscientious manner—working toward moral reforms. Some, however, were not interested in moral causes. With one hand held delicately to her brow in a fainting pose and the other clasped firmly around the butt of a .32 revolver, Vera Prosser is a prime example of how gender roles could be manipulated for morally reprehensible reasons—in her case, to get away with murder.

Vera Phillips was born in Cleveland, Ohio, in 1884 to an upper-middle-class family. Vera was a spirited young girl who grew into a great beauty. Described as an "attractive woman of prepossessing figure, large gray eyes, and a lovely face crowned by an abundance of raven tresses," Vera was pursued by many of Cleveland's most eligible bachelors. Her reputation for exacting tastes in clothing and jewelry show that she enjoyed the chase. At the age of nineteen she was married, but the union, and the husband, were short-lived.

Not much is known about Vera's first husband—a man she referred to only as Mr. Clark. The couple was married only a short time before they separated. Vera remained in Cleveland and Mr. Clark moved on to California, where he died under "mysterious circumstances." Vera recovered quickly from the blow of her ex-husband's death. Less than a year later, in April 1905, she married a dashing young man by the name of Reese Prosser. With his good looks, fine clothes, and flashy lifestyle, Reese Prosser caught the eye and the heart of the lovely Miss Vera.

Reese, the only son of a well-to-do coal family from Lisbon, Ohio, had a reputation for living hard and fast. So much so that his family cut him off financially, refusing to support his wayward lifestyle. Reese was forced to find gainful employment as a traveling car salesman. This proved the perfect career for Prosser—he could drive beautiful new cars, wine and dine clients, and flirt with women all over the Midwest.

Reese's "high life" did not end with his marriage to Vera. His work kept him on the road for months at time, and Vera often accompanied him. The couple would stay in fancy hotels and indulge in fine food and wines—often to excess. The Prossers became infamous for their spending sprees and alcohol-fueled fights.

It was not long before the romance soured. Reese began to leave Vera behind in Cleveland and head out on the road alone. He would be gone for weeks on end, and when he came home he was often drunk and quarrelsome. Following one particularly vicious night of fighting, a neighbor woman reported entering the Prosser apartment to find Vera sobbing, clutching a handful of her own hair. Reese had sheared off several clumps of Vera's beautiful raven locks while she slept. This was only one salvo in a series of pitched battles waged between Vera and her husband.

In 1908 the Prossers moved to Seattle, where Reese had secured a position with the Winton Motor Company as a salesman for the

Northwest region. Reese enjoyed his new playground. In fact his antics in towns across the Northwest—including Butte, Helena, and Missoula—earned him the title of "high roller." Reese and Vera quickly settled into their disturbed domestic routine as well, but in Seattle their inebriated rows became public spectacles. On one occasion Reese captured the limelight by climbing into a bathtub at the posh Rainer-Grand Hotel—fully clothed. He decided to take the plunge after Vera had commented on his disheveled appearance. The intoxicated twosome came to an impasse when Reese could not get out of the tub on his own accord and Vera could not assist him. Each time Vera tried to pull him out, Reese took a swing at her and fell back into the tub. The commotion they created finally brought the management to the room. Reese was hauled out of the tub and into a waiting police car. He was later released when Vera refused to press charges.

In April 1909 Reese failed to come home at a decent hour, and Vera took steps to ensure that he could not go anywhere for a while. After Reese staggered through the door, Vera helped him to bed and waited for her husband to pass out. She then stripped Reese down to his socks and left . . . with his clothes. The *Seattle Times* reported that Reese claimed his wife locked him up in a local hotel, removed his clothes, and then sold them, compelling him to remain in his room until the landlord "came to his rescue with garments borrowed from other guests."

This was not the only instance where Vera got the best of Reese. The *Times* reported that on several occasions the volatile Miss Vera had physically attacked Reese. On one occasion she broke a vase over Reese's head in a popular restaurant. Another time she ripped an expensive topcoat off his body as he tried to attend a party. And on yet another occasion she attempted to throttle him in front of a full courtroom where, fittingly, the couple was answering charges of disturbing the peace. In the last case Vera had to be physically restrained by a bailiff.

According to friends and coworkers Reese was becoming increasingly frightened of his wife—so much so that he risked plunging to his death from a rooftop to avoid a conflict with her. Again, the *Seattle Times* ran a story about the couple's turbulent relationship:

> Mrs. Vera Prosser . . . caused a sensational scene yesterday afternoon in the law offices of Thomas MacMahon. Mrs. Prosser held a vigil outside the office entryway for over an

hour. She was only outwitted by Mr. Prosser when he dropped from MacMahon's office window to a court roof, scrambled through an open window in a neighboring office, and sprinted down the backstairs of the building.

The following day the superior court issued a restraining order against Vera, enjoining her to "desist from attacking, beating or in any way molesting Reese T. Prosser." Reese then filed for divorce, claiming that Vera's temper had "made his life one long lingering burden without cessation or relaxation." The beleaguered husband then fled town until the scheduled court date.

When a *Times* reporter asked Vera for comment, she quipped, "It was Wine, Women, and Whiz Wagons that led to this slap at connubial bliss"—thus countering Reese's statements with her own accusations. She described Reese as a philanderer who posed as a popular vaudeville actor of the same name and enjoyed taking beautiful young women on joyrides in his company cars. She further stated that Reese's excesses had dissipated her fortune of some $15,000 (money she had recently inherited following the death of her wealthy father), leaving her penniless.

Despite her public outrage, and threats of a countersuit for nonsupport, Vera did not even attend the court hearing. The divorce was granted, without contest, on May 18, 1910. Two weeks later, on May 31, Reese Prosser was called to Ohio to receive a sales award from the Winton Company headquarters in Lisbon. He set out by train with his boss and a coworker in a private car. Unbeknownst to Reese, Vera boarded the express in Spokane.

The ex-Mrs. Prosser traveled in the standard coach, where she spoke freely with her fellow travelers about her marital woes. She became especially friendly with a man named C. C. Arlington, telling him not only intimate details of her married life with Reese but also of her desire to reconcile with her ex-husband despite his harsh treatment of her. At one point Vera grew so despondent she declared in a loud voice, "I'd like to throw myself in there (referring to the river she viewed from the train), but first I must get to him." And she did! Arlington later reported that Vera, returning from a short absence, announced to the travelers in the car, "My husband and I have made up; I am going to see him." As she turned and left, all within the car nodded their approval.

The reconciliation appeared to go quite well. A porter recounted

Woman Who Will Fight
Sensational Divorce Case

The Sea

20 PAGES. SEATTLE, W

Mrs. Vera Prosser.

WOMEN OBJECT | **QUEEN ANNE DOG**

MRS. PROSSER DENIES USING ANY VIOLENCE

Wife of Automobile Salesman Declares That Wine, Women and Buzz Wagons Led Husband From Home.

SAYS HE BOASTED OF HIS JOYRIDES

Wore Swell Clothes When Courting Her, but She Had to Foot Bills for Them After Marriage.

REESE T. PROSSER.

"WINE, women and whiz wagons led to this slap at connubial bliss," declared Mrs. Vera Prosser today, after indignantly denying that she ever offered violence to her husband, Reese T. Prosser, a salesman for the Winton Motor Car Company.

"It is absolutely false that I kept my husband a prisoner in the office of Attorney T. H. McMahon," said Mrs. Prosser. "The story is ridiculous and would be funny if I were not heartbroken. My husband has filed suit for divorce. The papers were served on me today. According to the story published Saturday, my husband asserts I made his life one long, lingering burden without cessation or relaxation. That is

NORTHERN MEI MAY REACH OF CONT

Alaskans on Board N ern Say Fairbank doughs Meet Wit pected Success on I

CLIMB 12,000 FEET WITHOUT DIFI

Months of Prepara Final Dash Near According to Word by Incoming Alaska

ALASKANS arriving he Northwestern last n that the Fairbank Kinley expedition has met pected success and they b likely that by this date, the North America's highest pea conquered by the little ban Tanana miners.

This is the party organiz Lloyd, Bob Horn, Harry K Charley McGonigle—all "sc and men known throughout for trail hardihood and dar left Fairbanks early last wi tablish supply stations on grades of the mountain fo pose of making an early su for the summit.

From the advices sent bac banks last month it now ap the climbers found condition encouraging than expected a account decided to attempt th fully three months ahead o originally considered. In a back to Fairbanks by a hu days ago Lloyd told of havi the 12,000-foot level without

"From the surveys we hav pleted," he wrote, "we belie found a route by which we the summit without having come any very serious diff will be steep climbing over o but that is the only prospe on which we will have to

From the 12,000-foot leve of about 16,000 feet, Lloyd there is a perpendicular wall rock that reaches so far to as could be seen. This seemed to bald the mountain with a great band, was the on ble barrier that had been en

From Lloyd's note it was to that the final lap of the would be undertaken about of March. Allowing a wee for trail location the party o climbers should now be in from which they will reach t the continent," or which will it to be inaccessible save by

450,000 NEW YORKER

delivering three drinks to the couple in Mr. Prosser's private compartment. In each instance the man and woman were increasingly cozy—in fact with the last drink Reese was partially undressed and had Vera perched on his lap.

But when the train stopped at the small mining town of Libby, Montana, Vera left the train, ostensibly to send a telegram, but did not reboard. C. C. Arlington, who turned out to be a retired policeman from Philadelphia, became suspicious and went to locate Mr. Prosser. When no answer came from Mr. Prosser's door, the porter was called and the door unlocked. They found Reese lying dead on the floor of his compartment in a pool of blood, dressed only in an unbuttoned union suit. He had a single fatal bullet wound to his left temple.

Mr. Arlington got off the train to find Vera. At the Libby station he found her calmly waiting to board a westbound train to Sand Point, Idaho. A search of Vera's belongings unearthed $5,000 in cash, several hundred dollars' worth of jewelry, and the murder weapon—a stylish pearl-handled .32. Vera was escorted to the Richard's Hotel in Libby, as the newly finished Lincoln County Jailhouse did not have accommodations for women. A coroner's inquest was scheduled for June 3.

During the inquest the prosecution easily showed that Vera should be held over for trial. C. C. Arlington; George Lindsay, a porter on the train; and Reese's traveling companions George Williams and A. G. Shaeffer were key witnesses. Their statements revealed that Vera was the only person on the train who had both the motive and the opportunity to shoot Reese.

Arlington stated that Mrs. Prosser had confessed not only to shooting Reese but also to a failed attempt to poison Reese's alcohol. George Lindsay testified that Vera had paid him to spy on Reese and tell Vera when he was alone. He also described the compromising scene in Reese's compartment when he delivered drinks to the couple. George Williams and A. G. Shaeffer discussed the violent scenes Vera had made at the Winton offices in Seattle and her repeated threats to get even with Reese. The inquest found probable cause and set the trial for August 15.

Throughout the inquest Vera was described as "self-possessed and cool," refusing to testify until she could secure an attorney. Despite claims of destitution Vera was able to secure as counsel a man described as "one of the foremost criminal lawyers in Montana," Senator Thomas Long of Kalispell. From the moment that Vera retained Senator Long, her demeanor changed. She became demure, helpless, and sweet. With her able counsel, her mesmerizing beauty, and most importantly her considerable acting skills, Vera was able to draw public attention away from the brutality of her crime and to establish herself as the true victim. But Vera played to a receptive crowd. Libby at the turn of the twentieth century was a small mining community where men outnumbered women two to one. In addition, it was common knowledge that Montanans were not predisposed to convicting women—a fact that a local official in Libby at the time of the trial echoed by stating, "We have never convicted a woman for a capital offense, and I doubt we will."

It is not surprising then that during the three months she stayed in Libby awaiting trial, Vera Prosser was treated like a celebrity. Local newspaper articles read more like society pages than coverage of an accused murderer. The *Libby Western News* reported:

> Mrs. Prosser chats pleasantly with everyone who is allowed to see her and seems to be in quite a happy frame of mind. . . . When out with her guard Mrs. Prosser spends the time in collecting four leaf clovers. She now has over two hundred of them. She files her precious omens of good luck away between the leaves of magazines.

During this time Senator Long did his part by announcing to the press that any statements made by Vera following her arrest—including her confession—were the rantings of a hysterical woman that should not be given credence.

The tactics seemed to work. The people of Libby were soon of the opinion that Vera should not be convicted of murder. Deputy Sheriff and Jailer Schanck remarked, "The sentiment here has crystallized into this, that if she were abused by Prosser as she says . . . she was justified in killing the brute." By contrast, Montanans outside Libby were not convinced. The *Whitefish Pilot* remarked, "According to reports Mrs. Prosser stands a good chance of getting off with no punishment at all . . . all on account of the hypnotic influence she holds over men. We suggest that the members of the ladies aid send their most attractive members as lobbyists to the trial to see that justice is doled out on the square!" The *Eureka Journal* published a disdainful little ditty aimed at Vera entitled the "Lady of the Forest Reserve":

You can kill your husband, if you've got the nerve, down in the blooming forest reserve . . . [for] Lincoln County is rich and she will pay. The prison cell is not a fit place to hold a lady of comely grace. A guard by day and a guard by night . . . and the board of the lady of the forest reserve . . . [for] Lincoln County is rich and she will pay. The pungent mocha and Java blend, ice teas, buttermilk and drinks without end—soft boiled eggs and mountain trout, the whole bill of fare [the county coffers will pay] for the daring lady with her .32 who shot her hubby through and through . . .

The fact that Eureka had recently lost the race for county seat to Libby might have something to do with the terse tone of the article!

Vera's trial began on August 15, with Senator Long and Mrs. Prosser working in tandem to present the defense. Long's opening statements portrayed a woman broken down by the abuses of a brutish husband, a woman who, under the strain of that treatment, snapped and shot her tormentor. Vera underscored Senator Long's arguments with her erratic behavior in the courtroom. While the charge was being read, Vera "collapsed, and with her head resting on her arms moaned, sighed and in convulsions rose and ran for the door," where Bailiff Brockman "held her languishing form on his arm." The court took a recess until Vera was well enough to return. Led in by a nurse, Vera was "pale, rigid and stared straight ahead" when she returned to the courtroom.

Vera was "taken ill" on several other occasions during the trial, including sobbing hysterically as her counsel asked an insanity expert to describe Vera's mental state during the shooting. In addition, Long was able to procure testimony from former neighbors, a doctor who treated Vera for injuries inflicted by Reese, and several hotel clerks who witnessed Reese's inebriated tirades. The most sensational statement, however, came from the insanity expert. He testified that "after satisfying himself with Vera . . . Reese turned on her and called her a vile name and grabbed her by the throat. It was then that Vera took a gun and shot him." The overall effect of these witnesses was to show that Reese Prosser was a drunken lout of man who probably deserved the bullet.

The prosecution, on the other hand, did not fare as well. Sheriff Maiden rested his case on written testimony from the coroner's inquest. None of the most powerful witnesses—Arlington, Lindsay, or Williams—could be secured to testify at the trial. In addition, the prosecutor failed to reveal Vera's bad behavior—including her bouts with alcohol, her earlier attempts on Reese's life, or the restraining order placed on her by the Seattle court. He also failed to question Vera's story about the shooting. For instance, why was Vera carrying a gun? Why were there no signs of struggle either in the sleeping car or on Vera? How did Vera manage to place a bullet at point blank range into the temple of a man who was attacking her?

The case took three days to be heard. The jury was out overnight. The verdict was acquittal by reason of self-defense. Vera's response to the acquittal was to hoist up her well-tailored skirts, run out the court-house door, and yell to the assembled crowd of well wishers, "I am a free woman." She then left Libby almost immediately. The *Western News* described her melodramatic departure: "Standing upon the rear platform of the last car on train no. 3, Mrs. Vera Prosser waved a tearful farewell to the fine people of Libby."

Vera did not, however, leave the limelight behind in Libby. She stopped in Spokane to celebrate with friends. The widow told a *Spokesman Review* reporter that she was thankful for her freedom, adding, "I have received several telegraphic requests for my services on stage. I think I have a good stage presence. I may work up a vaudeville sketch to recoup my finances." She never did take up acting—at least on the stage.

Vera's life following the murder trial reveals a woman much less wholesome than the one shown to the people of Libby. Mrs. Prosser pursued a nefarious career that took her all over the West Coast—to Portland, Seattle, Los Angeles, and San Francisco. Going by various aliases, Vera repeatedly ran at odds with authorities for domestic disturbances and financial scams—including a sensational extortion case in Los Angeles for which she served eighteen months. While serving that jail sentence in November 1913, Vera sent greetings to her "friends" in Montana:

> Mrs. Vera Scott, in jail in Los Angeles . . . said today that she was the woman who killed Reese Prosser in a railroad sleeping car [as the train passed into Montana] in 1910.
>
> [She went on to say] that after treating her royally while she was nominally a prisoner in Libby, a jury chosen from among the miners of the vicinity acquitted her in six minutes.

In addition to her failure to keep within the bounds of the law, Vera could not keep a marriage on the straight and narrow. She married a salesman named Lloyd Scott just a few months after the completion of the trial in Libby. He divorced Vera less than a year later on the grounds of cruelty.

In fall 1914 Vera married for the fourth time. Her newest love, George Murphison, was a San Francisco pool hall operator who was rumored to be hiding out from police on an old murder charge. Domestic bliss was not to be for Vera. On the evening of September 22, 1914, after only a few weeks of marriage, the quarrelsome couple came to a bloody truce—Murphison fatally shot his comely wife and then himself. The newspaper coverage of the murder-suicide seems a fitting epitaph for Vera.

Prior to her tragic death, Vera had "pursued a spectacular career" in Los Angeles, Portland, and Seattle. She was convicted of vagrancy in Los Angeles, where she extorted money from wealthy citizens in Los Angeles and Pasadena. She boasted that although she had landed in Los Angeles with only $3.00, she was able to amass a fortune of $60,000. The *San Francisco Chronicle* reported:

> Her career since moving to San Francisco had been just as squalid. Under the various names of Phillips, Murphy, Murphison she and . . . her husband moved from one hotel to another, as management refused to countenance the behavior of the pair and their frequent quarrels.

Vera was only thirty years old at the time of her death.

Vera Prosser's short life was a tempestuous and often violent affair. Perhaps she deserves pity instead of disdain. Reese was obviously abusive, cruel, and obnoxious. But then so was Vera. Given their volatile mix of alcohol, arrogance, and jealousy, it is not surprising that their relationship ended in bloodshed. Vera was a jerk not because of her murder of a worthless husband but because of her behavior just prior to, during, and after the murder trial. Her actions reveal not a desperate and abused wife but an arrogant and manipulative woman who used all her charms to get away with premeditated murder. For while we cannot know what passed between Vera and Reese in the sleeping car, it seems likely that she either wanted her ex-husband in her arms or in a box. It appears she got both.

Perhaps we should ask ourselves why? It seems clear that at every turn, Vera was able to garner public sympathy—primarily by acting the part of a frail and overwhelmed woman. That Vera succeeded in this ruse is testament to the fact that despite the rise of the New Woman many Americans still held to nineteenth-century views of womanhood.

Vera Prosser's life seems a twisted union of frailty and victimhood, strength and abuse. Her life was lived in patterns—patterns of deceit, manipulation, and violence. Patterns that led her to murder Reese Prosser ... patterns that allowed her to spellbind the people of Libby ... patterns that allowed her to walk free from a murder charge ... and ultimately patterns that brought her to an early grave.

Sources

Vera Prosser and her outrageous behavior might well have remained a hidden story were it not for Rose Goyen, a high school teacher in Libby. She told the story to Dave Walter, who passed it on to me. Thank you to both for leading me to Vera.

Vera Prosser's exploits were often front-page news featured in several newspapers: The *Western News* (Libby), 1910; *Whitefish Pilot*, 1910; *Kalispell Journal*, 1910, 1913; *Kalispell Bee*, 1910; *Eureka Journal*, 1910; *Butte Miner*, 1910; *Missoulian*, 1910; *Seattle Times*, 1910; and *San Francisco Chronicle*, 1914.

Legal records were also very useful in following this story. The office of the Clerk of District Court for Lincoln County provided copies of court documents filed in *State of Montana vs. Vera Prosser*. A special thanks to Nadine Pival and Irene Cadwallader for their prompt and courteous service!

For more information on the role of women in early-nineteenth-century America, see Dorothy Schneider and Carl Schneider, *American Women in the Progressive Era*, 1900–1920 (Anchor, 1994); and Steven Mintz and Susan Kellog, *Domestic Revolutions: A Social History of American Family Life* (Free Press; 1989).

Felony and the Fairer Sex: Violence and Perception in the Cases of Edith Colby and Bessie Smith

Jodie Foley

AMERICANS LONG HAVE HELD CONFLICTING VIEWS OF WOMEN WHO COMMIT violent crimes. In the Victorian Era society vilified violent women as unnatural beings who betrayed the innate gentleness and moral purity of their gender. Females who committed such crimes "unsexed" themselves and thus deserved neither special consideration nor treatment. By contrast, violent females in the Progressive Era were perceived as victims whose pure nature was only temporarily sullied by the crimes they committed. They were fallen women capable of reform and worthy of compassion. Despite the divergent interpretations, there is a common theme. At base is the belief that women were *naturally* incapable of violent crime.

In Montana's criminal justice system this belief, coupled with the deplorable conditions found in the women's ward in Deer Lodge, translated into a reluctance to sentence even violent female criminals to serve hard time. While it is true this reluctance provided compassion to many deserving women, it also provided sanctuary for some truly rotten females. Edith Colby and Bessie Smith are cases in point. In the winter of 1916 each made headlines in western Montana newspapers for committing bloody crimes. Edith Colby, a political reformer and Thompson Falls newspaperwoman, shot an unarmed man. Bessie Smith, a cook in a women's lying-in hospital, brutally attacked an ex-lover. In both cases the women claimed that abusive treatment and temporary insanity drove them to violence. This defense was not chosen by accident. Both women, and their defense teams, knew that by presenting themselves as "good women pushed to do bad things" they could gain sympathy—and possibly acquittal.

An only child, Edith Colby was born in Dunberton, New Hampshire, in 1872. According to family members Edith was a high-strung girl with boundless energy. As a young woman she took an interest in Republican Party reform efforts. In her thirties Edith was devastated by a failed romance and decided to leave the East Coast to seek better opportunities in the West.

Why she chose Spokane, Washington, as her haven is unknown, but Edith arrived in the Lilac City in 1910. She quickly found work as a proofreader for the *Spokesman Review* and jumped into local politics. Between 1910 and 1915 she was appointed assistant city labor agent, made a bid for a city commission seat, worked on a congressional campaign, and served in the local welfare league. In all cases Edith drew support from women's groups, who saw her as a moral voice in politics.

Her personal life was likewise rich. She even found love again, becoming engaged in 1913 to Dr. H. Hilscher, proprietor of the Spokane children's sanitarium. By all appearances Edith's life was back on track. But appearances are often deceiving. Edith Colby had a dark side: an angry, dishonest, self-absorbed, and violent side that soon came to overshadow her life. On one occasion Edith's temper nearly resulted in a public whipping. Collecting signatures on a street corner in downtown Spokane, Edith was insulted by two young men who called her a streetwalker. In a fury Edith demanded that a male coworker take a whip to the young men to defend her honor. When he refused, it took several other coworkers to keep Edith from turning the whip on him!

In addition to blind rages, Edith delighted in humiliating those who crossed her. Her beloved Dr. Hilscher felt the sting of her scorn when he broke off their engagement and married another woman. A few weeks following his nuptials, Edith approached her ex-fiancé on a busy street in Spokane, wrapped her arms around the startled doctor, and cooed, "Well, hello there, daddy!" She then proceeded, to the delight of the crowd, to kiss him violently on the lips. Prying his former lover's arms from his neck, the scandalized Hilscher forced his way through the crush of people and fled.

Even Edith's reform work became tainted. Following what was described as a "personality conflict," Edith was fired from her position as an assistant labor agent. A few weeks later, in a clear ethical breach, Edith opened her own employment agency, despite the fact that many agencies were being investigated for graft.

Edith's dreadful behavior continued through 1915, reaching a bloody climax in August 1916. Following her breakup with Dr. Hilscher, Edith's life was in a shambles. She lost her fiancé, her job, and, because she lived at the children's sanitarium, her home. She tried to find employment again with local newspapers but was told she needed a union card. Because of her reputation in Spokane, it was not likely the union would issue Edith a card, crippling her ability to find work.

Angry and humiliated, Edith decided to leave Spokane in May 1916. She responded to an advertisement for a newspaper job in Thompson Falls, Montana, and was hired by J. Manier and A. S. Ainsworth, editor and owner, respectively, of the newly established *Independent Enterprise*. The *Enterprise* was an alternative to the *Sander's County Ledger*. Thompson Falls was a town deeply divided in the early twentieth century, and each newspaper served as a mouthpiece for different political factions. The *Ledger* represented those who opposed Prohibition and were pro-development, while the *Enterprise* spoke for those who supported Prohibition and were angered by the city's domination by wealthy outsiders. The rift was played out weekly in the editorials of each paper—and into the fray stepped Edith Colby.

In her efforts to report stories for the *Enterprise*, Edith conducted interviews with community leaders including A. C. Thomas, chairman of the Sanders County Republican Party and a strong supporter of the *Ledger*. He had successfully avoided Edith for several months, but on August 28, 1916, she cornered him on Main Street. During the unpleasant exchange, Thomas vented his spleen at Edith, saying that he refused to talk to anyone who worked for a paper that told lies. Then he suggested that Edith was brought to Thompson Falls for more than her journalistic skills. Thomas told her that "I have seen women like you before, but here we keep them in the red-light district." Mr. Thomas walked away, leaving a fuming Edith Colby behind him.

Edith spent the next few hours in a highly agitated state, sharing her outrage with anyone who would listen, including coworkers, the clerk of court, a local shopkeeper, and even her doctor. All sympathized with Edith and suggested that she confront her accuser. Edith decided she would get her apology and concocted a plan. She then took her nightly dose of chloroform, grabbed a bottle of whisky, and headed off to bed.

At ten o'clock the following morning, Edith walked onto the porch of the Hotel Ward, where she knew Thomas would soon be passing. She receded into the shadows of the outside staircase and waited. As Thomas drew near, she stepped out to block his path and demand an apology. Thomas refused and attempted to pass, but Edith stepped into his path once again, this time with a .38 revolver in her hand.

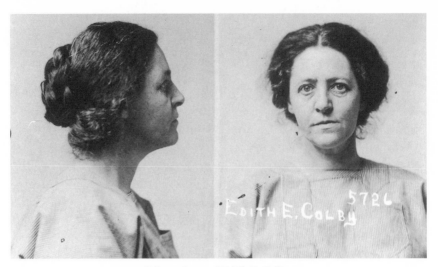

Prison photo of Edith E. Colby.
MONTANA HISTORICAL SOCIETY, HELENA.

Without further comment she fired twice at Thomas, mortally wounding the man. Hearing shots, a bystander tried to come to Thomas's aid. Edith, however, turned the gun on him and told him to stand back. He retreated. Edith then turned back to her task, fired two more shots at the wounded man, put the gun in her purse, and proceeded down the street to her office. Thomas, who had taken two bullets to the stomach, staggered to the nearest business and collapsed. The local doctor determined that Thomas had to be rushed by train to Missoula for treatment or he would die.

As soon as the train pulled out, Sheriff Hartman entered the offices of the *Enterprise* and placed Edith under arrest. As she was being led away, Edith turned to A. S. Ainsworth and demanded, "Well, what are you going to do about this?" When he responded, "I am not going to do anything about it. I do not believe in this sort of thing," Edith tried to lunge at him but, being restrained, instead spat, "You told me I could do anything I wanted to [to Thomas] . . . All right, I will fight this alone. You are yellow from head to foot." She was quickly removed from the premises but not before implicating her editor, Mr. Manier, who she claimed had told her to shoot Thomas because they needed the headlines! Neither man was ever brought to trial, but Edith was . . . for murder. Thomas died the following day.

The coroner's inquest found ample evidence to hold Edith over for trial. Eyewitnesses described the circumstances of the shooting. Co-workers described Edith's angry ranting, which included statements like "I am so mad I could kill Thomas" and "How far do you think I could take this?" The Cleres, owners of the boardinghouse where Edith roomed, identified the gun she used as one that had been stolen from their room. All of these circumstances showed probable cause and motive. The court set the trial for November 27.

For lead council Edith hired John T. Mulligan, the attorney on whose congressional campaign she had worked. Burton Kendall Wheeler, a promising young U.S. district attorney from Butte, led the prosecution. As attorney for the defense, Mulligan had a challenge before him. The shooting had occurred in clear sight of witnesses, and Edith's statements established a clear motive. Undaunted he set a two-pronged, if slightly contradictory, defense: First, Edith did not intend to kill Thomas; second, she was insane at the time of the murder.

To prove the latter Mulligan brought in a long line of witnesses from Spokane to expound on Edith's eccentric behavior. Friends described Edith's fits of rage and inappropriate public behavior. Her work associates described her ill-conceived business schemes, and an insanity expert described the effects of menopause on someone of Edith's age. She was just forty-four at the time of the crime.

Public responses during the trial show that the strategy was working. One newspaper reported that "a new tendency the state is striving to overcome is that of people in the audience, especially women, to laugh when points are made against the prosecution. So loud was laughter Saturday that Judge Clements threatened to clear the courtroom." Given this and general public sentiment against convicting women, Edith could have gained an acquittal—that is, if she had tried to substantiate her witnesses' claims. Instead, under cross-examination she repeatedly contradicted her own witnesses.

One witness pointed out several occasions where Edith reversed her stance on important issues during her city commission campaign. When the prosecution asked if she was aware she had done this, she replied, "Yes, but I thought the city commission race was a joke, so I did not prepare any statements and just said what came to mind"—so much for her devotion to public service.

She also contradicted witnesses who believed her odd business propositions were a sign of mental instability. Miss Ruby Drake testified that she held $1,500 equity in a home, but that Edith had tried to convince her to find buyers for it at only $500 and put her money into a business Edith was starting. When Edith was asked under cross-examination to explain why, she shrugged and stated, "I needed the money quickly and didn't see why I shouldn't try to get it." Edith was not so much mentally challenged as she was ethically bankrupt. She further hurt her case with statements that highlighted her outrageous temper. When a *Missoulian* reporter asked her why she confronted Thomas with a gun, she coolly replied, "I wanted to humiliate him; I wanted to see him run; I wanted to make him dance."

Perhaps the worst damage to the Colby defense came with Edith's courtroom behavior. On several occasions her temper flared; in fact, during the prosecution's closing remarks she exploded. Her former employer, the *Spokesman Review* reported:

> No sooner was the sentence out of the mouth of the attorney than Miss Colby sprang from her bench . . . seized the chair as if to attack and at the top of her voice shouted "That is all a lie. I will not stand for this." It took Mulligan and two others to remove her from the courtroom. Her screams resounded throughout the building long after the doors had been closed.

Following summation the jury was given instructions and sent to deliberate. After six hours of tense discussion and six separate votes, the jury returned its verdict. On the morning of December 7, 1916, Edith Colby was found guilty of the lesser charge of second-degree murder and sentenced to ten to twelve years in the state penitentiary at Deer Lodge.

Edith vowed that she had only just begun to fight. True to her word, with assistance from her mother and lawyer, she started a letter-writing campaign. The trio wrote to the prison warden, the governor, and the attorney general pleading for Edith's release. The letters alternately argued that Edith was framed, was insane, or was mistreated in prison. One letter even claimed that forcing her to room with black women was cruel punishment. Edith received a gubernatorial pardon in 1919, reducing her sentence to a minimum of five years. "Good time credit" cut that in half. On July 19, 1919, just two years and eight months after committing murder, Edith Colby was a free woman.

∼

At the same time that Edith Colby's murder case was a front-page story, a beautiful young woman named Bessie Smith made headlines of her own. Bessie was born in 1890 in Cadmus, Michigan. Her parents separated when she was quite young, leaving the family near destitution until her mother remarried. The relationship between mother and daughter was a stormy one, so Bessie left home at the age of eighteen. Working as a domestic, she made her way west, arriving in Montana in 1909. She lived in Bozeman and Three Forks before gaining employment as a cook at the Parker Maternity Hospital in Missoula in 1910.

Bessie was described as a lovely and slightly naive young woman who attracted the attention of many young men. Her heart, however, was reserved for one man: a rugged cowhand named Fred Huffington. Huffington "cowboyed" for the Waddington Ranch near Florence, Montana, and came into Missoula once a week to spend his paycheck and woo the fair Bessie.

It was an affair destined to end badly. Huffington was a lout, who falsely won Bessie's heart with promises of marriage. When pregnancy forced the issue, Huffington's love faltered, but Bessie was not dissuaded. Even when Huffington threatened to kill her if she did not leave him alone, she did not give up. She approached Huffington's employers who suggested that legal action might persuade him to do the right thing. Bessie went to Missoula County Sheriff R. J. Whitaker and told her tale of betrayal. Bessie first wanted to file a complaint of white slavery but could not; Huffington, while a cad, did not solicit Bessie's affection or offer her services to others. Bessie settled for a complaint of seduction and abandonment.

With complaint in hand, the sheriff, Bessie, and a deputy sheriff set out to arrest Huffington—ostensibly to force reconciliation. At the Waddington Ranch, the startled ranch hand was taken into custody without incident. He was placed in the backseat of the police car with the deputy sheriff. Bessie and the sheriff were seated in front.

Halfway through the return trip Bessie turned and offered her hand to Huffington, stating, "I just want to talk things out." Seeing something other than reconciliation in Bessie's eyes, Huffington shouted to the deputy, "I think she has something in her other hand!" Before the deputy could respond, Bessie pulled a revolver from her coat pocket and, steadying it on her shoulder, shot Huffington squarely in the mouth. Bessie then surrendered to the bewildered sheriff. Bleeding profusely, Huffington was taken immediately to St. Patrick's Hospital.

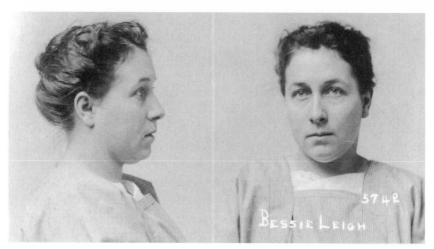

Prison photo of Bessie Leigh.
MONTANA HISTORICAL SOCIETY, HELENA.

But the drama was far from over. Once Bessie was taken to her cell, she announced she had taken strychnine and hoped to join her lover in death. A doctor was brought in to treat Bessie, who was declared out of danger within an hour.

The following morning, the *Missoulian* announced "Deceiver Shot by Anxious Woman." The article outlined the events of the previous evening and quoted Bessie as saying she didn't intend to kill Huffington but had taken the gun to defend herself. She believed that, "half-crazed with anxiety," Huffington might be "moved to violence by the appearance of officers." Between sobs she claimed, "I don't know what made my hand do it!" Despite the brutality of the crime, public sentiment was clearly behind Bessie. The *Missoulian* reported:

> She loved not wisely, but too well; that is all that really can be said against her. That is why she is in the county jail this morning recovering from the effects of a self-administered dose of strychnine, while Fred Huffington lies at St. Patrick's hospital wavering between life and death.

Within twenty-four hours of the dramatic shooting, suicide attempt, and arrest, however, the authorities were able to surmise that the sweet young woman named Bessie Smith was not quite what she seemed.

After making a few inquiries and interrogating Bessie, the police found that her first name was nearly the only thing Bessie had not lied about. Bessie Smith was actually Bessie Leigh, wife of Tilden Leigh, an inmate in the prison at Deer Lodge. Not only was she married but she had three children whom she had placed in a Helena orphanage. She was also no longer pregnant, as she had had an abortion two months prior to the shooting.

Bessie also lied about her relationship with Fred Huffington. Far from being an inexperienced ingénue, Bessie lived with Huffington, posing as his wife on a ranch in the Bitterroot prior to moving to Missoula. It also turns out she had a similar arrangement with a man named Stanley.

Having destroyed her claim of seduction, her stated reason for the shooting, the police began to piece together another motive—revenge and greed. Huffington not only had deceived Bessie about marriage plans but also, more importantly, about his finances. Huffington claimed that he held partial ownership in the Waddington Ranch and was preparing to sell it. On the night before the shooting Bessie learned the truth.

While the investigation went forward, Huffington succumbed to his wounds. Bessie now faced first-degree murder charges.

A perfunctory coroner's hearing, held on October 4, 1916, established that Bessie shot Huffington and that he died from the resulting wound. Trial was set for December 12. The court appointed Harry Parson as Bessie's attorney, and Missoula County Attorney F. C. Webster led the prosecution. While awaiting trial Bessie was held in the Missoula County Jail, but her defense attorney was not idle. In the eight weeks between the commission of the crime and the trial, Parson was able to gather public sympathy for his client.

The *Missoulian* printed letters from family and friends pleading for mercy:

Dear Bessie,

My sympathies are ever with you. It has often been in my thought that if the county had furnished you sufficient money to live on after I was sent here you would have been home with the children and this lamentable tragedy would have been avoided.

Signed your loving husband,
Tilden Leigh

Another letter written by Bessie's father, A. M. Gander, began with an excerpt from a poignant O. Henry tale called "The Guilty Party":

The story opens in the dingy interior of a tenement home ... at the window is a dirty unkempt man reading a newspaper. The daughter, an innocent youngster asks her daddy for a story. . . . "Go on out and play in the street," the father growls. . . . years later the girl kills her lover in a fit of jealous rage. The story should end here but O. Henry dreams he is in heaven and the case of the girl is called for trial. The celestial detective calls the girl a bad case . . . but [the divine defender] argues the guilty party was the man sitting in the window reading his paper.

The letter continued, outlining the sad life of his wayward daughter. Gander blamed Bessie's deviant ways on bad friends and meddling neighbors. The message to the potential jurors was clear: "This good girl was led astray by others. She deserves our pity and an acquittal."

When the case came to trial, Bessie pleaded not guilty by reason of temporary insanity, induced by a mixture of morphine and strychnine. Predictably, the defense and prosecution presented contrasting views of Bessie's motives in shooting Huffington. The defense presented an abandoned woman. Thinking she was divorced because her husband was a convict, Bessie sought a new spouse to provide for her and her children—and chose badly. Huffington used Bessie and then became abusive. Bessie turned to the authorities for help, but in a drug- and fear-induced state did not trust their ability to protect her and bought a gun for self-defense. The shooting, of which she remembered little, occurred in a morphine fugue that had made her unaware of what she was doing. Bessie therefore should not be held responsible.

The prosecution, on the other hand, portrayed Bessie as a cold-blooded killer, "driven by a man's scorn" to murder her lover. County Attorney Webster also implied that Bessie was an easy woman, who killed her lover "not because he had deceived and disserted her but because she could no longer hold him." The latter interpretation held increasingly more weight as the prosecution undercut Bessie's defense at every turn.

The drug-induced insanity defense was destroyed through the testimonies of Sheriff Whitaker, Dr. A. G. Fuller, and Dr. Pease. The sheriff described the calm and calculated way in which Bessie committed the crime: steadying the gun on her shoulder to avoid a wayward shot. He went on to argue that her demeanor was not that of one on morphine. Doctor Fuller testified that the amount of strychnine and morphine Bessie claimed to have taken would have caused convulsions and a coma. Further, Dr. Pease, who treated Bessie at the jailhouse, admitted that he took her claim of poisoning at face value, never testing to see that anything was present in her system. He also saw no effects of drugs the following day and concluded that she had not taken anything at all.

The final blow to Bessie's case came from her own mouth. During her incarceration Bessie confided to a female officer that she had planned to kill Huffington and would have taken another shot at him, but the deputy got in the way.

With so much evidence against her, there was little Bessie's defense attorney could do in the end but plead for mercy. This he apparently did with great skill. On December 17, 1916, Bessie Leigh was convicted of manslaughter. Judge Asa L. Duncan, in passing sentence, gave credit to Bessie's attorney for gaining the lower sentence. The judge specifically commended the attorney's passionate closing remarks in which he argued that Bessie should be allowed to leave Deer Lodge in the arms of her husband so that they could rebuild their broken family.

Like Edith Colby, Bessie Leigh served only a portion of her original sentence. Arriving at Deer Lodge in December 1916, Bessie was released in April 1919, after serving a total of two years and four months.

Edith Colby and Bessie Leigh had many things in common: Both were arrogant and self-absorbed; both were motivated by revenge to commit their crimes; both were aggressors in well-planned-out attacks; both manipulated the legal system; and both were convicted of lesser crimes and gained early release.

How did they get away with it? Perhaps the "chivalry" accorded these women by the law and public not only aided them in their defense but also facilitated their crimes. Why didn't anyone take Edith's ranting seriously? Why did Sheriff Whitaker take Bessie with him to arrest Huffington and then not even think to check her for weapons? The answer is simple: It never occurred to them to do so. Perhaps the mantle of shame can be shared among the various players in these two stories, including the men who abused and used these women and those in the system that allowed the women to take their revenge. Ultimately, however, Edith Colby and Bessie Leigh stand as the primary villains in their stories—each manipulated cultural views of womanhood to exact her revenge and pay little for her crimes.

~

Sources

I first came across the stories of Edith Colby and Bessie Leigh while doing research on women in Montana State Prison. Elaine Way, then curator at the Deer Lodge Prison Museum, graciously shared her expertise and research with me. A special thank you to Elaine! Those interested in learning more about women in Montana's prison can check *Record Series 197: Montana State Prison Records* (Montana Historical Society Archives, Helena, Montana). Also helpful was a report by Susan Byorth, *History of Women Inmates: A Report for the Criminal Justice and Corrections Advisory Council* (Department of Corrections Web site, 2002); and an essay by Paula Petrik, *Beyond the Bounds of Misery: Montana's Female Prisoners in the 1930s.*

The specifics of both Edith Colby's and Bessie Leigh's criminal cases were obtained primarily through newspapers: *Spokesman Review*, 1916; *Sanders County Ledger*, 1916; and the *Missoulian*, 1916. For additional information on Edith's case see *Record Series 76, Montana Attorney General Records* (Montana Historical Society Archives, Helena, Montana).

Those wanting more information on women in America's penal system should check out the following: Estelle Freedman, *Their Sisters' Keepers: Women's Prison Reform in America*, 1830–1930 (University of Michigan Press, 1981); Nicole Rafter, *Partial Justice: Women, Prison, and Social Control* (Transaction Publishers, 1990); and Shelley Bookspan, *A Germ of Goodness: The California State Prison System*, 1851–1944 (University of Nebraska Press, 1991).

SELL AMERICA FIRST:
HOMESTEADING ERA PROMOTIONS
Lyndel Meikle

EARLY IN THE 1900S, THE GREAT NORTHERN RAILWAY ADOPTED THE SLOGAN "See America First," hoping to lure Americans to tour their own country instead of taking the traditional Grand Tour of Europe. This admirable sentiment was a new twist on the search for customers, which had begun some years earlier in a campaign that should have been called "Sell America First." Abandoned homesteads dot the West—mute testimony to the unscrupulous tactics of railroad land agents who lured homesteaders out to settle on land that could not be successfully farmed.

At first glance there appears to be a wealth of evidence of their deceit. The claims of the railroads were extravagant, often deceptive, and sometimes just plain false. The disaster that struck the homesteaders was tragic and undeniable. But trying to pin down the jerks in the case feels a bit like a game of "Where's Waldo?" After factoring in the various homesteading laws, the effects of World War I and its aftermath on the grain market, the weather, bad science, freight rates, the cost of wintering stock, upheavals in Europe, congressional investigations, investigations *of* Congress, and the frenzied finance of that day, it is no longer a simple case.

To start near the beginning, in 1830 there were 23 miles of railroad in America. A mere thirty years later, there were 30,000 miles. In another thirty years there were 164,000 miles; and in 1916, less than a hundred years after it all began, the building boom crested at more than a quarter of a million miles of track.

Bonds sold in America and Europe helped finance some of this building. Financiers gambled whole financial empires on railroad construction. But by far the most significant factor in the building of western railroads was the granting of public land to the railroad companies, the sale of which was to finance construction. This began in 1850 with the Illinois Central. In the early 1860s Abraham Lincoln granted more land to railroads than did any other president.

The construction of the Union Pacific led to the Credit Mobilier scandal, which involved a dummy corporation and the awarding—or low-cost sale—of railroad shares to certain key legislators.

Attempts by Jay Cooke to finance the building of the Northern Pacific would lead to the collapse of his financial empire, leading to the Panic of 1873 and the worst depression the country had yet experienced.

How closely the history of Montana is linked to the railroads is evident from the names of our towns. Frederick Billings of the Northern Pacific was chairman of its land committee. Cooke City was named for financier Jay Cooke. Hill County was named for J. J. Hill, whose Great Northern Railroad would eventually control the Northern Pacific as well. A few more towns named for and by our various railroads include Baker, named for the construction engineer of the Milwaukee Road, and Belgrade, a name contributed by a Serbian bigwig riding to Gold Creek with Northern Pacific president Henry Villard for the driving of the "last spike" on that line in 1883. Carter was named by the Great Northern to honor a U.S. senator, and Dillon was named for the president of the Union Pacific.

In a separate bit of public relations, the Great Northern named the town of Chinook, undoubtedly to back up its campaign to convince Easterners that winter temperatures in Montana were mild—but more on that later. One story that could be true claims that a town in northwestern Montana called Columbus demanded too much money for its land when it was proposed as a division point for the Great Northern. Jim Hill moved the division point to Whitefish and renamed Columbus, "Columbia Falls." It could be true—but it probably isn't. Then, to really complicate things, Stillwater, Montana, west of Billings, was the subject of confusion, as there was already a Stillwater, Minnesota. As a result, another railroad, this time the Northern Pacific, renamed Montana's Stillwater "Columbus."

This list of towns is impressive, but incomplete. What about Accola, Acushnet, Archer, Arnold, Ashmore, Austin, Barford, Barrows, Bascom . . . It's unnecessary to go through the entire alphabet, but the point is, dozens of towns sprang up across the state along the route of the railroads, wherever depots were established. But where are they now?

The first big push in land promotion came in the 1870s. The Northern Pacific had received a huge land grant of about forty-seven million acres along its route. It needed to sell land to raise money for construction of the line. Then it would need to find customers along the route. At that time, there was no prospect of business between northern Minnesota and Puget Sound except the mining communities of western Montana. Bringing in immigrants who would first purchase railroad lands and then use the railroad to ship agricultural products was a capital solution—that is, a solution that produced capital. The railroads also promoted the settling of homesteads on adjacent government lands.

First, of course, the railroads had to convince people that there were good reasons for leaving the civilized East and settling in a little known and nearly empty land. The railroads aimed early publicity at eastern landowners who wished to enlarge their operations but found land prices in their home area too high. Then there were renters who could be convinced that they could buy their own, cheaper western land—and that with the income they would derive from the fabulously productive new soil, they could pay off their loans in just a few years. Whole "colonies" were recruited. Religious groups founded communities, secure in the belief that their righteousness would ensure success. After all, if God could temper the wind to the shorn lamb, it should be a piece of cake to send more rain into arid country.

By 1872, just a decade after the discovery of gold and a decade before the Northern Pacific would actually complete its route, pamphlets promoting Montana were making the rounds. The railroad wined and dined newspapermen, treating them to excursions to carefully selected grant lands and then sending them back home to write seemingly unsolicited platitudes about the "New Northwest." Exhibition trains displayed the bountiful harvests of the West back East, and—everywhere—the printed word bragged of this new "Nile of the North," this "Mediterranean of the Northwest."

In 1883 the Northern Pacific printed nearly two and a half million pamphlets, circulars, and folders for distribution in the East and in northern Europe.

The building of railroads was not straightforward, and there's no need to go into all the problems of the late 1800s, including frequent bankruptcies and delays caused by irksome little details such as the desire to illegally cross reservation lands, cutthroat competition, and congressional investigations. A few examples of the often amusing and occasionally outrageous ploys will suffice.

As early as 1873, one of Billings' associates wrote that whether

Montana—The Land of Independence map with text produced by the Great Northern Railway in 1917 as part of its "See America First" campaign.

MONTANA HISTORICAL SOCIETY MAP COLLECTION.

they wanted to acknowledge it or not, "the question of climate is a sockdalager [a telling blow], and this obstacle . . . can only be overcome by convincing people that, in spite of the long and cold winters, they can live comfortably and make money on the line of the Northern Pacific."

The promoters did better than that. They did away with our long and cold winters. "The climate of Montana," wrote the Northern Pacific in the early 1890s, "is perhaps the most delightful of any state in the Union. Its moderate altitude imparts an exhilarating quality to the air, the proximity of the mountains insures cool nights during the hottest periods, while the chinooks effectually prevent the cold of winter from getting any firm hold, and sweep away in a few hours the snow that in other localities would require many days of sunshine to melt." Other literature claimed that tuberculosis was cured in Montana's clean, dry air, along with all other respiratory complaints.

West of the 100th meridian, which runs through the Dakotas, lies what was once known as the Great American Desert. Having disposed of our cold winters, the railroads next sought to eliminate the problems of raising crops where there was not sufficient water to do so. Even such a renowned western surveyor as Ferdinand Hayden (of Yellowstone's Hayden Expedition) was not immune to wishful thinking. In a report to the Secretary of the Interior, he wrote, ". . . the planting of 10 or 15 acres of forest-trees on each quarter section will have a most important effect on the climate, equalizing and increasing the moisture and adding greatly to the fertility of the soil . . ."

Especially charming was the theory of Charles Dana Wilber, an amateur scientist and—incidentally—land speculator. Plowing was thought to increase rainfall. As he phrased it, "Not by any magic or enchantment, not by incantations or offerings, but, instead, in the sweat of his face, toiling with his hands, man can persuade the heavens to yield their treasures of dew and rain upon the land he has chosen for his dwelling place." Or, in the catch phrase of that day, "Rain follows the plow."

Since the introduction of this theory coincided with a number of years of better-than-average rainfall, it gained some acceptance, but the inevitable dry years turned the theory—and many homesteads—to dust. Railroad claims of 24 inches of precipitation annually in the Billings area had to be revised down to a more realistic 15 inches.

The railroads entered the twentieth century with their appetite for settlers unsated. Not only was there still grant land for sale and free government homestead land unclaimed, but many of the sales of the previous century had been abandoned by bankrupt homesteaders and could now be resold. The recruitment of immigrants continued.

Some of the more extravagant rhetoric had been toned down. For example, in a booklet issued by the Northern Pacific Railroad before 1896, it was claimed, "Competent irrigation engineers have figured that there are 40,000,000 acres of irrigable land in Montana." In a 1910 address given in Bozeman, Northern Pacific Railway president Howard Elliott proudly announced that there were five to six million irrigable acres. Nearly a century later, crops were harvested from fewer than two million acres of irrigated land in Montana, and while more land might respond to irrigation, the water rights battles that would ensue make increased irrigation a mere fantasy.

So, if rain didn't follow the plow, rainfall was less than had been claimed, irrigation projects were bogged down in disastrous funding efforts, and it turned out to be cold in the winter, how could the railroads lure more people to Montana?

The next big sales pitch brought forth a theory that sounded scientific and reasonable, particularly when it was backed with the entire propaganda machine and enormous budget of the railroads. And it *was* an enormous budget: In his 1910 address, Northern Pacific president Elliott claimed that the Northern Pacific had spent $8,000,000 to date advertising western lands.

By this time, the Northern Pacific and its rival, the Great Northern, had become one, although they maintained the fiction of being held not by a common corporation but by individual investors who just happened to be the same people. This was to avoid the risk of Congress accusing them of unfair competition—or lack of it.

The new sales technique acknowledged low rainfall and unirrigable land, but solved the problem by showing that farmers didn't need as much water as they had thought. With Montana's mild climate, plowing could begin as early as January or February. It was wonderful, they claimed, how most of the state's rain came in the months of May, June, and July, as soon as planting was finished. Then, fortunately, the rain would stop until the crops were harvested and return briefly in the fall to rehydrate the ground. The trick, they explained, was to save every possible drop of moisture that fell.

One of the most famous proponents of dryland farming was Hardy Webster Campbell. So well known was his propaganda that methods of dryland farming came to be known as the Campbell

System, even when they bore little resemblance to his theories.

In a nutshell, Campbell claimed that by plowing deeply into the prairie sod, solidly packing the subsoil, and maintaining a layer of constantly cultivated dust on top, every available drop of moisture could be conserved. His program focused on small grains, which were easily cultivated. He also advocated summer fallowing of fields every three years, leaving the plowed soil bare to absorb extra water for next year's planting.

The method did conserve moisture, though not enough to save crops in drought years. And when there was a heavy rain, it saturated the subsoil, trickled down to salts that had lain undisturbed for millennia on the bedrock, dissolved them, and carried them along until they found a place to emerge as saline seep. The battle against saline seep continues to this day.

That fine layer of dust on top was supposed to be maintained as a sort of thermal blanket that would hold moisture in the subsoil. Since the dust was constantly "fluffed up," it wasn't compact enough to allow water to move up through it by capillary action. This was supposed to cut down on evaporation, but since the layer was not compacted, drought and wind sent it blowing away.

That was the very layer that contained organic nutrients that nourished the prairie grasses, which had supported bison for centuries. Professor Thomas Shaw, the Great Northern's tame agricultural expert, had the solution for this problem as well.

Diversification, he claimed, would make the soil inexhaustible. There should be a three- to five-year crop rotation, and not only crops, but livestock should be raised, as the manure produced, when tilled back into the soil, would restore its nutrients. He established demonstration farms, gave seminars, and boosted dryland farming throughout the country. In this, he had the wholehearted financial support of railroad baron J. J. Hill, and this is where an enthusiastic "exposé" of railroad promotional tactics runs into a slight check. Hill seems to have actually believed Shaw. Did that make him a "jerk" or a victim?

Here is where Montana Historical Society archives come to the rescue. Among the boxes of promotional pamphlets put out by the railroads, the booster literature printed by the towns, personal recollections, reference books, and so on, there are five reels of microfilm of Great Northern records. In December 1909, just as the scene was being set for the disaster that would hit the plains after World War I, Dr. Cyril G. Hopkins, professor of agronomy and chemistry at the University of

Montana homestead, n.d.
PHOTOGRAPH BY EVELYN CAMERON. MONTANA HISTORICAL SOCIETY, HELENA.

Illinois, typed a twelve-page letter to Hill, explaining in great detail why Shaw's system was wrong.

As to fertilizing the soil with manure, he pointed out that animals are not made of nothing—that their bodies are made up of nutrients taken from plants grown in the soil, and that even if all the wastes are recovered, and "about one-half of the value is contained in the liquid excrement, which is almost as difficult to recover as spilled milk," the combined output (you should pardon the expression) of every domestic animal in America would barely be enough to take care of the soil nutrient needs of Illinois.

Hill responded, disagreeing, and Hopkins wrote back, nearly pleading with Hill to listen. Hill stuck with Shaw.

Shaw was wrong. Hill was wrong. But agriculture was an evolving science. The points Hopkins made seem perfectly obvious today, but would they have been as obvious to Hill and Shaw? It seems as though they should have been, but Shaw had a career and a propaganda empire invested in his system. Accepting Hopkins's science would mean a loss of face and income.

Hill had land to sell. He had a railroad to run. He needed settlers and he needed customers, and Hopkins didn't offer him any easy way to get them.

Hill didn't live to see his "Nile of the North" turn to dust. He died in 1916. The drought had not yet established a death grip on the deeply plowed fields. Land prices, inflated by speculators, had not yet plummeted. The wheat harvest had not dropped from twenty-five bushels per acre to five. The end of World War I had not yet sent inflated prices from $3.26 a bushel to $1.72 in a mere seven months.

But the immigrants saw it all. Between 1919 and 1925, two million acres went out of production; 11,000 farms were gone; 20,000 mortgages were foreclosed. Half of all Montana farmers lost their land, and the value of farmland dropped 50 percent.

Many publications tell the stories of those farmers. In Milton Shatraw's book *Thrashin' Time,* his father, Edward Shatraw, described his feeling about the land:

> You know, when I first went into Teton County, I could ride horseback all day with the buffalo grass and wild hay brushing my stirrups. The streams ran full, and cattle grazed everywhere. But the drought and dry-land farming has changed everything. Now you see farm machinery abandoned in the fields. The houses are deserted, the people gone. The thin topsoil has blown away, leaving the land empty and bare, and everywhere the everlasting tumbleweed rolling across the fields, banking up against the rotting buildings, and caught in the tangled barbed wire fences. It's like the end of the world.

It may have been the end of his world, but some homesteaders managed to hang on. Optimistic newcomers arrived. New methods were tried. Mistakes were corrected. Today agriculture is as vital to Montanans as the air they breathe—that mild air, warmed by the chinooks, containing just the right amount of rain at just the right time, curing our respiratory problems, and never bringing blizzards, hail, excessive heat, or inconvenient frost. Hardy Webster Campbell wrote in 1909, "I believe of a truth that this region which is just now coming into its own is destined to be the last and best grain garden of the world." He had a point. Wheat is vital to Montana's economy, and as Montanans are fond of pointing out, it really is the "Last Best Place."

~

Sources

Much of the material for this chapter came from microfilm and pamphlet collections at the Montana Historical Society, including *MF 449: The Great Northern Railway Company Papers;* pamphlets entitled *Irrigation in Montana, Montana for the Farmer, The Problem of Land Settlement,* and *Through the Fertile Northwest;* and *Montana Agricultural Statistics, 1867–1976.*

Those interested in more information should refer to *Montana: A History of Two Centuries;* "Pearl Danniel, Homesteader in Big Dry Country" (*Montana: The Magazine of Western History,* Fall 1996); and *It's Your Misfortune and None of My Own* (University of Oklahoma Press, 1991). For more information on homesteader experiences in Montana, see *Homesteading in Montana: A Family Album* by Percy Wollaston (Penguin, 1997); and *Bad Land: An American Romance* by Jonathan Raban (Vintage, 1997).

Legislative Lunacy: A Sampling of Montana's Looney Laws and Legislative High Jinks

Lyndel Meikle

THIS ESSAY IS ABOUT STUPID LEGISLATION—LAWS THAT MADE IT INTO THE books and those that did not. These are the kinds of laws that make us chuckle, like "It is illegal for married women to go fishing alone on Sundays, and illegal for unmarried women to fish alone at all." It is unclear if such a law was ever actually on the books in Montana, but reviewing the *Montana Codes Annotated,* a researcher can find an ample supply of other lunacy. In fact there is such a wealth of legislative material in the Montana Historical Society archives that it is easy to get sidetracked. Searching through the State House and Senate records for Montana Territory (1864–1889), it's easy to get distracted by memorials and resolutions sent to the U.S. Congress. Each session, the territorial legislature made requests of Washington. Many fall into identifiable categories: imperialism outside Montana's borders, imperialism within the borders, and basic bigotry. Some are funny; others are infuriating.

Take imperialism outside the borders. In January 1872, the territorial legislature told the U.S. Congress that it would be a wonderful idea to set aside an extraordinary area of geysers, boiling springs, mud volcanoes, burning mountains, lakes, and waterfalls. This was a good idea. Yellowstone National Park was created by an act of Congress in 1872, but not the way Montana's Territorial Legislature had planned. They had meant for Congress to cede the new park to Montana, not form a national park. They tried again in 1874, pointing out that Montanans properly appreciated the park and that they'd be able to protect it better if it were in the territory's jurisdiction. They "earnestly prayed" that "so much [of Yellowstone] as now lies within the Territory of Wyoming be detached there from and be attached to the Territory of Montana." Nice try. In the long run, Montanans have dealt with the fact that 91 percent of Yellowstone is in Wyoming by simply believing that it is all in Montana.

In 1877 Congress heard from the territory again. This time it wanted to annex that part of southern Idaho through which a railroad might reasonably be expected to pass on its way to Montana. The theory was that by helping the railroad reach Montana by way of Idaho, Idaho would be enriching itself, with no payback from Idaho to Montana. Therefore, it would be only fair to give the land to Montana. By this reasoning, Montana's borders would soon have extended to New York.

Then there was what might be called imperialism *within* the territory and state. Between 1864 and 1921, there were at least thirty-five requests to reduce the size of American Indian reservations or open them to white settlement and mining. More than once, Montana legislators stated that a particular piece of reservation land was valueless to the Indians but rich in agricultural land or precious metals. A sample of this hypocrisy was expressed through Senate Joint Memorials 1 and 2, from the sixth legislative assembly in 1899. On page 153 legislators asked the U.S. Congress to "Make it unlawful for Indians resident upon reservations in the State of Montana to ever at any time or for any purpose leave or be found off their reservations and to enact such measures as will stringently enforce such legislation." On the very next page, there was a request for a special Indian Commission to be appointed to facilitate the speedy opening of the Flathead Indian Reservation for white settlement and cultivation.

There are many other examples of odd legislative requests that do not fit into a neat category. In 1917 a memorial was sent by Montana to the U.S. Congress to stock the National Bison Range with reindeer. A 1917 resolution urged newspapers to eliminate duplication *and* repetition in the printing of news by discontinuing all daily papers or changing the same to weekly papers and substituting them with one or two large daily papers. There may have been a more sinister motive here than mere economy. One or two daily papers would have been easier to censor and manipulate than many.

There was a 1921 request to "pass an enabling act by which the people of Eastern Montana may segregate their territory and frame their State Constitution and thereby become a sovereign State of the Union."

Leaving the memorials and resolutions and getting back to the laws, one of the first that catches the eye is the crime of embracery. Though this conjures up intriguing visions of illicit hugging, it turns out to be jury tampering.

Divorce laws provide some amusing legal conundrums. In territorial days, if a man cheated on his wife, she could get a divorce. If she cheated on him, he could get a divorce. If they cheated on each other, neither one could get a divorce. If they colluded to get a divorce by one party pretending to cheat, and such deception was discovered, they could not divorce. And if a faithful spouse forgave an erring spouse once but decided that a repeat offense was carrying things too far, it was too late. By forgiving, the innocent party had become a party to the guilty party's first offense, and no divorce would be granted.

A law in early territorial days that definitely qualified for the jerk category barred Blacks, Indians, and Chinese from being witnesses when parties to the action were white.

Guns were outlawed in 1911, and confiscated weapons were to be brought to a magistrate, who would see that they were immediately destroyed. This might have been interpreted as a violation of some Constitutional right, but the "victims" of the law were too young to do much about it. It was cap guns that had been outlawed.

The next few examples could come under the heading of "They needed to make a *law* about that?" A proposed 1911 law stated: "It shall be unlawful for any sheriff, constable, police officers or any persons charged with the custody of any one accused of crime, of whatever nature, or with the violation of a municipal ordinance to frighten or attempt to frighten by threats, torture or attempt to torture, or resort to any means of an inhuman nature, or practice what is commonly known as the 'Third Degree' in order to secure a confession . . ." And early in the 1900s it was made ". . . unlawful for any person, firm, company or corporation now operating, or who shall hereafter operate a boarding house in connection with their general business, either directly or through others, to compel an employee to board in such boarding house against his will."

Early territorial law contained a startling bit of prejudice. Within the legal definition of kidnap, the legislature deliberately excluded the Chinese from the definition of those who could be kidnapped. Given the rampant anti-Chinese feeling in the entire country at that time, this is not entirely surprising, but it is difficult to pin down exactly when the law was revised. By 1901 the peculiar wording of the original law had been amended to include all people.

The samples of legislative lunacy provided thus far are really just a warm-up for the activities of Montana's 1890 Legislature.

Working back through the records to the 1890 Legislature, a

peculiar problem emerges. There is no record of the 1890 Legislature. There is no House Journal. There is no Senate Journal. There are no laws. We know it did occur because on November 16, 1889, Montana newspaper headlines shouted the happy news:

ADMITTED!!!

Montana became a Sovereign State of the Great Union Yesterday. To her sisters in the glorious Union of states, Montana, the brightest gem in the diadem of the nation, sends greeting.

Montanans quickly elected state senators and representatives, and someone who signed his letter to the editor with, "A Law-Abiding Citizen" announced in the *Yellowstone Journal:* "I shall be much disappointed if, in the organization of the legislative assembly . . . there are any revolutionary proceedings on the part of any member of either house of that body."

The author of that article was doomed to disappointment.

Controversy began right away because of a temporary precinct that had been set up to accommodate workmen building the Homestake Tunnel near Butte, in Silver Bow County: Precinct 34. The precinct had voted heavily Democratic, and fraud was charged. Among other things, it was alleged that the votes had been cast in alphabetical order of the voters' names—something the Republicans found suspicious. Despite the small number of voters in this precinct, the votes were important because whichever side won would determine the control of the House. Without the Silver Bow delegate, the House was evenly split. The Republican-controlled Board of Canvassers told the county clerk to issue certificates of election to the Silver Bow Republicans. The Democratic county clerk refused to do so.

To further complicate matters, the state senate was also evenly split, with eight Democrats and eight Republicans. However, any tie vote in the Senate would be decided by Lieutenant Governor John Rickards, a Republican.

Governor Joseph Toole, on the other hand, was a Democrat, and while he was powerless to affect state senate votes, he vehemently supported the Silver Bow Democrats.

Roughly five dozen men, many of whom had previously worked together to hammer out a constitution and win statehood for

Montana, were unable to work together because—in those days—the selection of the two senators to be sent to Washington, D.C., would not be done by popular vote but by a vote of the legislature. With the Senate evenly split, whichever party controlled the House would select the senators.

This part of the fiasco is well known. Montana could hardly hush it up. After a mortifying delay, the Republicans sent Wilbur Fisk Sanders and Thomas C. Powers to Washington, and the Democrats sent William A. Clark and Martin Maginnis.

What is less well known is the shambles the two parties made of Montana's first few years of statehood, but it's all there in the Montana Historical Society archives: newspaper accounts, the diary of Senator Cornelius Hedges, the tactfully written biographies of the participants, even the absence of the legislative books of 1890 from their otherwise complete records. They all tell the story.

In November, Governor Toole designated the Lewis and Clark County Courthouse as the place for the representatives to meet. The rumor circulated (denied by Toole) that only those holding certificates of election from county clerks would be recognized. It was claimed that those holding certificates from the state canvassing board would be turned away. Fearing that the Republicans representing the disputed Silver Bow seats would be ejected, the Republicans met elsewhere, and for the entire ninety-day session, the two sides of the House met separately.

The Democrats called the Republican gathering the "Rump House," which sounds a bit rude, but the dictionary reveals that rump means, "a legislature having only a small part of its original membership and so lacking authority." The Republicans got even later by calling Clark and Maginnis the "rump senators."

The Democratic state senators, knowing they couldn't count on a majority in the House unless their Silver Bow delegation was seated, refused at first to take the oath of office, believing that once they did, they would have no way to prevent the Republicans—with Lieutenant Governor Rickards's tie-breaking votes—from taking over.

Republican Senator Fisher got into a swivet, shouting dire warnings through the press that unless the senators fulfilled their appointed tasks, "No criminal prosecution can be properly had and criminals would be turned loose upon the community and order would be

1890 Montana Democratic Senate members (back row from left to right): Dr. Wm. Parberry, R. G. Redd, Wm. S. Becker, Jos. A. Baker, (front row from left to right) Wm. Thornton, C. J. McNamara, C. W. Huffman, D. J. Hennessy.
MONTANA HISTORICAL SOCIETY, HELENA.

turned to chaos." Had he taken the trouble to read the new state's constitution, he would have known that all the old territorial laws would remain in force until altered, repealed, or expired.

Matters weren't helped any when Governor Toole ordered all locks changed on the legislative building, although he insisted this was only done to ensure proper care of the rented facility.

Finally allowing themselves to be sworn in twenty-four days after the session began, the Democratic senators still maintained the impasse by refusing to answer roll call, thus depriving the Senate of a quorum.

At this point, Montana made it into the U.S. history books because of a precedent-setting move by Lieutenant Governor Rickards. In mid-December he declared that simply failing to answer roll call did not mean the Democratic senators were absent. He decreed that if they were there, they could be seen, and if they could be seen, a quorum was present and a vote could be called—a vote that everyone recognized would favor the Republicans. A few weeks later in Washington, D.C., U.S. Speaker of the House Thomas B. Reed followed Rickards's lead to break an impasse in that body, and a long-held tactic of obstruction that had been cherished by both parties became a thing of the past.

Meanwhile in Montana, time dragged by. It was not until January that each side of the Senate named its own two senators to go to Washington. The Democratic *Daily Independent* didn't seem particularly enchanted with the Republicans' top senatorial pick, Wilbur Fisk Sanders. A lead article ran, ". . . How truly he stands for this latter day republicanism, for the party in its degeneracy, in its disregard of popular rights, its contempt for an honest ballot, its centralizing tendencies, its caesarism, its alliance with monopolies, its conscienceless attitude toward all public questions."

The Republicans were equally rude about the Democratic choice, announcing in the *Herald*, ". . . It is presumed that Mssrs Clarke [sic] and Maginnis will go to the expense in time and money of making a trip to the national capitol. Doubtless they will have a pleasant trip, be the first to congratulate Senators Sanders and Powers on taking their seats in the Senate and learn a great many things they never dreamed of before." The Republican-controlled U.S. Senate seated Sanders and Powers.

After the Rickards "visible quorum" decision, the Democrats absented themselves completely from the Senate chambers. On the eighth of January, Senators Baker and Parberry were hauled into the chamber by the sergeant-at-arms. By January tenth, the daily *Herald* dared hope that the deadlock was broken. It wasn't.

The separate but equally useless Houses of Representatives blundered on, passing no laws, unable to resolve the question of the disputed seats, and generally embarrassing the young state. By the end of the first week in February, the *Herald* was comparing the status of the government to Nero fiddling while Rome burned.

The Democrats still refused to appear in chambers, and an angry Lieutenant Governor Rickards gave orders that they were to be brought in. Suddenly Helena was too hot for the absentees, and they blew town.

On February 8 the papers announced that Undersheriff Parker, who had been sent to Glendive to bring Senator Becker back, would be charged with kidnapping. Republican Senator Cornelius Hedges wrote in his diary, "Great day in senate. Senator Becker brought back." The next day he wrote, "When we met today found that Becker had skipped. All confusion and rage again." The rest of the Democratic senators, fearing to be dragged back like Becker, didn't slow down until they were out of state, and even that didn't reassure them. Rumors circulated that they would be pursued with out-of-state warrants. Senators Hoffman and McNamara reportedly fled to Canada. Becker is alleged to have described his midnight flight as "One flew out of the cuckoo's nest."

Finally, the third week of February, the expiration of the ninety-day term brought the whole farce to an end, and it can fairly be said that it ended with a bang.

To celebrate the end of the session, the Rump House had a party during which members "humorously" tossed firecrackers at one another. Later that night, a wayward spark, which had apparently smoldered in a wastebasket, set the Rump House on fire. Luckily, no one remained in the building, or the "Rumps" might have made ashes of themselves as well.

~

Sources

There is no suggested reading for this particular jerks story because the House and Senate Journals for Montana's first state legislature in 1890 don't exist. However, researchers using the collection at the Montana Historical Society will find many articles of interest in the newspapers of the day. The library does have the journals of all the territorial sessions leading up to statehood and all the state sessions following that first, chaotic year. They provide endless history and unwitting humor along with ample cause for both pride and chagrin.

Montana Wastewater Woes: Going with the Flow
Lyndel Meikle

RESEARCHERS TRACING THE HISTORY OF SEWAGE HAVE A PROBLEM . . . THERE is way too much information about this rather unsavory and unsanitary subject. In fact there is probably more information available than most of us want to know.

The tributaries of human's toxic flow reach back into biblical times. One of the oldest sources on environmental quality is the Old Testament. In the beginning, of course, there was a lot of clean water in the world and not many people. However, as they went forth and multiplied, so did their by-products. In Deuteronomy 23:12, Moses told the people that when they camped at night, "thou shalt have a place also without the camp, whither thou shalt go forth abroad; and thou shalt have a paddle upon thy weapon; and it shall be when thou wilt ease thyself abroad, thou shalt dig therewith, and shalt turn back and cover that which cometh from thee." Thus was recorded one of the earliest documentations of human litter boxes.

Further research reveals that around 700 B.C., Babylon had a sewer 3 feet high, 164 feet long, and vaulted over with bricks. Even earlier, around 1,700 B.C., there were masonry sewers in Crete, including one with shafts to the fourth story of the palace at Knossos. Water was flushed through these ventilated sewage systems to enable them to more readily empty into nearby rivers and streams. That was one of the most persistent misconceptions causing the pollution of waterways. It was long held that flowing water would purify itself. The belief persists today, although Giardia has long infected mountain streams.

Society was on the right track in the days of Roman domination. Aqueducts as long as 40 miles brought clean water into cities to be used for drinking, bathing, cooking, and flushing sewers. Of course the Romans dumped raw sewage directly into the nearest flowing water source, but their love of bathing and their engineering skills meant that they were less vulnerable to typhoid, one of the chief evils of pollution by "nightsoil."

With the end of the Roman Empire, this healthful lifestyle came to a gradual end. Bathing came to be considered a sign of Roman decadence. Filth was a symbol of humble piety. Through the Middle Ages and into the Renaissance, open sewers, infested with rats and carrying along rotting food as well as other filth, were common. The Great Fire of London in 1666 may have saved more lives than it cost, since it at least temporarily cleaned the streets of offal and vermin.

As early as 1850, chlorine was used to disinfect pump houses in London. However, it would be half a century before its use became common. Meanwhile, filtration of water through sand and dumping of sewage into the nearest flowing water remained the most common "treatments."

One charming development was the increase in sewage farms, where sewage was used to irrigate crops. One poetic advocate of such farms tried to overcome the public's natural repugnance with this little poem:

> *Dear People! thus to fill my maw,*
> *By outrage of just Nature's law!*
> *If you but us'd your city's filth,*
> *To fatten crops, and feed their tilth,*
> *Till Nature turning "vile" to "good"*
> *Returned your waste in fruit or food!*
> *Your farms and fields would gain in wealth,*
> *Whate'er your city wins in health,*
> *And lustier crops and lengthening lives*
> *Would prove how sense with science thrives.*

American historians have revealed that only a short time before the American Revolution, public "facilities" were commonly provided for men only. Often women were simply supposed to exercise control until they got home . . . or stay home. Intrepid researchers have also informed us that toilet paper was invented in the mid-1800s. According to one source, prior to that time outhouses in coastal areas were commonly equipped with mussel shells. But one of the best tidbits on this subject is a story about a rancher who wrote to Sears, Roebuck to order toilet paper. They wrote back to say he'd have to provide them with the catalog number. He wrote back to say that if he'd had the catalog, he wouldn't have needed to order the toilet paper.

The typhoid bacterium was identified and described in the 1880s, and thus the source was found for outbreaks of the deadly disease. Of course it would be nice to be able to put the blame on one of the most common carriers of the disease, the housefly. But the fly was merely the means by which the infection was spread from one human to another. Typhoid is a disease of humans. The housefly, being more manageable than city councils, voters, budgets, and mayors, took most of the blame at first. Across the nation, programs were launched to eradicate the fly. A contest in Salt Lake City resulted in nearly 4,000 quarts, an estimated forty-eight million flies, being captured.

Montanans gleefully engaged in the assault on the housefly. Early in the 1900s, Dr. Tuttle of the Montana Board of Health published this bit of doggerel in his monthly health newsletter:

The dirty rascal plants his feet on filth, and then on what you eat; He cake-walks through a garbage can, and lights at once on a frying pan; he gathers poison with his toes, and leaves it on the baby's nose; He's on the friendliest of terms with all the death-dealing germs. One dirty, nasty, little fly can spoil a whole day's milk supply. The pesky, buzzing, mean galoot, exists but to befoul, pollute; He isn't very hard to please—He's happy if he spreads disease. Make friends if you wish of a rabid dog, a rattlesnake or a slimy hog; But every time you see a fly, biff him squarely in the eye.

Montana's attitudes about dealing with human sewage were very similar to the prevailing attitude about range animals. Back East, farmers had to fence their stock in. Out West, people had to fence other people's stock out.

In the same way, Montanans felt it was the responsibility of each city to filter pollution out of its water supply—and not that city's responsibility to keep its sewage from polluting cities downstream. This was practical only if the city took its water from the headwaters of the stream. The farther downstream you were, the worse the water was.

Chlorination began to be common in the United States at the beginning of the 1900s but suffered setbacks when too much chlorine made water unpalatable and too little made the process ineffective. Properly used, chlorine had several advantages. It killed bacteria and helped oxidize decaying vegetation, so the palatability of water was sometimes improved. In fact, filtration and disinfection of drinking water is credited in a large part with the 50 percent increase in life expectancy in the 1900s. Mortality rates from typhoid dropped from 25 per 100,000 people in 1900 to virtually none in the entire U. S. population by the middle of the century.

So by 1900 Montana officials knew what caused typhoid and how it spread. They also knew how to treat the problem, but did they do what needed to be done?

They tried. In 1907 the Montana legislature passed a sewage treatment bill to protect the people of the state. It gave the Health Department oversight of waters used for domestic purposes and made clear that ". . . no sewage, drainage refuse or polluting matter, of such kind . . . as . . . will corrupt, pollute or impair the quality of the water of any spring, pond, lake or stream used as a source of water or ice supply by a City, Town or public institution or water or ice company for domestic use, or render it injurious to health, and no human excrement, shall be discharged into any such stream . . . unless such sewage, . . . shall have been purified so as to render it harmless."

Howls of protests rose from municipalities that foresaw budget troubles ahead. In "Young Men and Filth," Dr. Spencer Shropshire of Helena wrote that Miles City sued the Board of Health, and the first finding was in the city's favor, using the Western water use doctrine of "first in time, first in right." The Montana Supreme Court disagreed, finding that the requirements of public health rated higher. But, it continued, a community could discharge raw sewage into a stream provided that no community downstream used the stream as a domestic water supply.

The City of Missoula complained, "Even before the Missoula River reaches Missoula, it is so polluted that it cannot be used for domestic purposes; therefore it seems to us an unnecessary hardship if we are required to purify our sewage at a great expense when there is absolutely no benefit to be derived from it. There is no chance of this river ever being used for domestic purposes, either now or in the future." Judge Woody asked, ". . . isn't there a probability that Plains might someday become a city and want to use the water from this river?" "It would be so expensive," was the reply, "that I do not consider it probable. At any rate, *we* would be willing to take the risk."

The judge decided that the city could dump raw sewage if it could prove that not one family from Missoula to the Montana border used the water for domestic purposes. Beyond Montana's border was of no concern—to Montana. In November 1909 the board approved Missoula's request.

Clancy had a bit more trouble trying to convince the board to allow continued pollution. The fact that the governor of Montana lived downstream may have had something to do with that.

The particular problem at Clancy was two sanatoriums. In the board minutes from April 1908, they noted, "The excreta and everything from all the sick people at Clancy goes into the stream, then the stream of that water goes directly into the big tank from which so many people drink the water. The tanks on the railroad are filled with this water, and the people who drink the water become sick after they leave Clancy, without knowing the reason." Dr. Tuttle explained that typhoid germs could exist in a river as far as it could flow in twenty-five days. Appalled, the governor said, "Then Helena could be infected!" Dr. Knowles replied that the same applied to all rivers in the state, but since typhoid was known to be present in the waters at Clancy, the board ordered them to take action on a new system immediately. Maybe the basic law of the West should be amended to "Always drink upstream from the herd . . . and the governor."

In 1911 the Twelfth Legislative Assembly weakened the law. It took some authority away from the board, and a crippling phrase was added: "A city or town shall not be prohibited or enjoined from discharging its sewerage into a river or body of water unless such sewerage so pollutes the waters thereof as to be dangerous to public health." Outbreaks of typhoid throughout the state caused the original act to be reinstated—six years later.

Meanwhile, Montana's drinking water and Montana's sewage flowed on as one. Most cities unconcernedly sent their waste downstream, but in 1914, when the City of Cut Bank submitted the plans for their drinking water facility, they neglected to mention that they were taking their water from a creek below the town—and below their sewer. They had several cases of typhoid in 1916. The problem occurred off and on, and in 1920 newly elected Mayor Purcell wrote to the State Board of Health. "Some time ago," he said, "you suggested that a chlorination plant be installed . . ." and asked for the board's advice and assistance. Twenty-four years later, the City of Cut Bank wrote to the board again, saying, "Among the recommendations that you make is one that consideration be given to the purchase of a [chlorination] plant . . . where can we make a purchase of such a plant? Will you kindly give us some help on this?"

Harlem complained for years about the sewage coming downstream from Havre and Chinook. Havre was very reluctant to comply with recommendations and—later—with laws. In 1905 the *Havre Plaindealer* noted with relief that a bill had failed to pass which would have required settling tanks be installed by cities dumping their sewage into a stream. "Had the bill become law," the editor noted, "it would have put the city of Havre to the expense of putting in settling tanks at a cost of several thousand dollars. In as much as Chinook, the nearest town on the river, is more than 50 miles by the river from this city, such a precaution was unnecessary and the passage of the bill would have worked nothing but hardship on this city."

In 1916 a young Harlem businessman was stricken with typhoid, and a Harlem physician was quoted in the *Harlem News* as saying, "if he dies, Havre will have killed him . . . as definitely as if they placed a rope around his neck and hanged him to a tree."

The next year the clean water law was strengthened again, but Havre was not yet convinced of the need to treat their water. Seventeen years later Harlem filed a complaint against both Havre and Chinook. Both cities were ordered to cease and desist dumping raw sewage into the Milk River, but a further perusal of the minutes of the Board of Health reveals that two years later, Havre and Chinook were proposing dumping more raw sewage into the river. Four years after filing their original complaint, Harlem's woes increased when they began receiving the foul-smelling waters of the sugar refinery at Chinook.

Harlem made its complaint against the Utah-Idaho Sugar Company in March 1938. In April 1939 the board made recommendations to the company, which it did not follow. Finally, two years after the complaint was filed, the company was ordered to discontinue putting its waste into the river until it could provide an auxiliary water supply for Harlem.

Eleven years later, and forty-three years after the first Montana laws against dumping sewage were enacted, Havre began complying with the law.

Havre may have been the longest holdout, but most cities fought what they deemed a needless expense. In 1940 Huntley Project, downstream from Billings, complained about the sewage Billings was dumping in the Yellowstone. Billings may not have responded immediately because they were too busy complaining about the sewage Laurel dumped into the Yellowstone.

Two years later, in the midst of World War II, Billings told the board that they might have to wait on a new sewage plant because of the "present emergency," but they promised to be ready "as soon as it could be constructed economically."

Happily for those who did not want to go through life boiling water, the problem began to resolve itself in 1950 with the passage of Montana's Water Quality Act. Further improvements came with the 1972 Montana Constitution and the 1974 Federal Safe Drinking Water Act. Today no one in Montana should have to worry about safe drinking water.

No one *should* have to worry, but only in the past decade, citizens of Butte were under a "boil order." Recent problems have—literally—surfaced throughout Montana in sewage systems that are now fifty years old. That's a mere drop in the slop bucket compared with the sewers of Knossos.

If it's hard to pin down exactly who the "jerk" is in this chapter, it may be as cartoonist Walt Kelly's "Pogo" observed: "We have met the enemy, and he is us." In 1931 educator Richard Tawney observed that, "it is not till it is discovered that high individual incomes will not purchase the mass of mankind immunity from cholera, typhus, and ignorance, . . . that slowly and reluctantly, . . . society begins to make collective provision for needs which no ordinary individual, even if he works overtime all his life, can provide himself."

As this chapter has revealed, there is a virtual flood of stories about the problems of maintaining clean water in Montana. Havre, the stories reveal, was once declared an outlaw city because of its refusal to treat its sewage. Environmentally aware Missoula once tried to justify polluting the Clark Fork River. And Cut Bank deliberately violated one of the most basic Western maxims: "Always drink upstream from the herd."

In any event, from the vaulted sewers of Babylon to the septic systems of unincorporated new Montana subdivisions, it's plain that if people want pure drinking water, they'll *all* have to pay the piper.

~

Sources

The Montana Historical Society archives hold many original documents that were used in preparing this chapter, including records of discharge of biological wastes into all Montana waterways. These papers may be read in the research room of the Society's library. It is further recommended that if the reader wishes to continue drinking water, it is better not to know too much about the subject.

INDEX

About the Authors

Jon Axline earned an M.A. in American history from Montana State University in Bozeman in 1985. Since 1990 he has been employed as the historian at the Montana Department of Transportation in Helena. Jon is currently the manager of the department's highway historical marker program and supervises its historic roads and bridges program in addition to answering the myriad questions that arise about the department's history. He is a coauthor of all three volumes of the Helena local history series, *More from the Quarries of Last Chance Gulch* (1995, 1996, 1998). He has also published articles about scenic U.S. Highway 91 (1998), the Montana, Wyoming & Southern Railroad (1999), and Thomas Francis Meagher (2003). A volume about Montana's historic bridges is forthcoming.

Kansas native **Ellen Baumler** is a fourth-generation Jayhawk and earned her Ph.D. in medieval studies from the University of Kansas in 1985. She has been the coordinator of Montana's National Register sign program at the Montana Historical Society since 1992 and is currently the society's interpretive historian. Ellen is the author of *Spirit Tailings* (MHS Press, 2002); coauthor with *Independent Record* editor Dave Shors of *Lost Places, Hidden Treasures* (Farcountry Press, 2002); and editor of *Girl from the Gulches: The Story of Mary Ronan* (MHS Press, 2003). Ellen is a frequent contributor to *Montana The Magazine of Western History;* "Devil's Perch," her study of Butte's red-light district, received the magazine's Vivian A. Paladin Award for best article of 1999.

Jodie Foley was born and raised in Missoula. She attended the University of Montana, studying at the undergraduate and graduate levels from 1983 to 1990. The Montana Historical Society Archives hired her in the summer of 1990, and she was promoted to her current position of oral historian and archivist in 1993. Jodie is coauthor of *Speaking of Montana: A Guide to the Oral History Collection of the Montana Historical Society* (1997); contributing author to *Speaking Ill of the Dead: Jerks in Montana History;* and a recurring presenter at the "Jerks in Montana History" sessions of the annual Montana History Conference. Her contributions to this volume stem from ongoing research she is conducting on women in the Montana State Prison.

Kristin L. Gallas was born and raised in Vermont. She received a Secondary History and Theatre Education degree from the University of Vermont and a Masters of Arts in Teaching in Museum Education from George Washington University. Kristin moved to Montana in 1998 to assume the position of education officer for the Montana Historical Society, a position she held until 2004. She is currently the Director of Education and Interpretation at the USS *Constitution* Museum in Boston, Massachusetts. Her piece on Toussaint Charbonneau is an endeavor to have fun with the Lewis and Clark Bicentennial commemoration.

Angie Gifford was born and raised in Helena, Montana. She attended both local high schools and Carroll College. At Carroll she studied history under the fine tutelage of Dr. Robert Swartout and Father Greytak. Angie went to work for the MHS Library in the fall of 1995 and for seven years served as "genealogy specialist." In that position she met people from all over the country and heard many wonderful family stories . . . many of which she then proceeded to prove wrong! When patrons walked into the library and told these stories they would inevitably end with, "What else can you tell be about my great-grandfather?" Angie would politely reply, "Well, about all we know for sure is they're dead. Let's see what else we can find." What a great conversation starter! Angie now works for the Montana Department of Transportation in the director's office as an information specialist.

Lyndel Meikle was born in Helena, Montana. A national park ranger, she began her Park Service career at Yosemite National Park and worked at Fort Point and Alcatraz before transferring to Grant-Kohrs Ranch National Historic Site in 1976. Her published works include *Very Close to Trouble: The Memoir of John Francis Grant* and several chapters in the first volume of *Speaking Ill of the Dead.* She has written the weekly column "Back at the Ranch" since 1982. Still a ranger at Grant-Kohrs Ranch, she also teaches blacksmithing at Powell County High School.

Dave Walter graduated from Wesleyan University (Connecticut) in 1965 and spent ten years working with Montana historian K. Ross Toole at the University of Montana in Missoula. He joined the staff of the Montana Historical Society in Helena in 1979, where he currently serves as the research historian. Since 1983 Dave has contributed a regular Montana-history column to *Montana Magazine,* and he is the author of several books, including *Today Then* (1992), *Montana Campfire Tales* (1997), *More Montana Campfire Tales* (2002), and *Christmastime in Montana* (2003). Dave's work on Montana's seemingly endless supply of jerks—including Simon Pepin, "Long George" Francis, James Brady, and the Montana Council of Defense—represents a lifelong commitment.